JOAQUÍN BOCHACA

FINANCE, POWER, and the CAPITALIST ENIGMA

OMNIA VERITAS®

Joaquín BOCHACA
(1931–2022)

Joaquín Bochaca was a brilliant Spanish intellectual, writer, journalist, translator, and historian. A man of vast learning, he studied history, law, and business. After living in England and France, he returned to Spain, where he produced a rich and original body of work. The author of more than 20 books and hundreds of articles, he is renowned for his exceptional erudition and his ability to tackle a wide range of subjects: history, economics, finance, psychology, and critiques of modern society. He also translated some thirty works by major authors into Spanish and Catalan. Until the end of his life, at the age of 91, he remained an active, ironic, and rigorous thinker, appreciated for his independent spirit and his profound knowledge of the 20th century. A cultured and prolific figure in contemporary Hispanic thought.

La finanza y el poder – El enigma Capitalista
1975-1977

Finance, Power and the Capitalist Enigma

Translated and published by Omnia Veritas Limited

OMNIA VERITAS®

www.omnia-veritas.com

FINANCE AND POWER

Cover: The symbolism of the dollar is clearly visible. Note the star formed by smaller stars above the United States coat of arms, as well as the symbolism on the left: a pyramid and a triangle with the suggestive inscription "New Order of the Ages"

* * *

THE THEFT OF THE CENTURIES

"Let me control a nation's money supply, and I care not who governs it."

Meyer Amschel Rothschild

"I fear that the man in the street will not like to know that banks can and do create money. The volume of money in existence varies only with the action of the banks in increasing and reducing their loans. Every loan or overdraft creates money. And those who control a nation's credit direct the policy of its government and hold in their hands the destiny of the people."

Reginald McKenna, Member of the House of Commons; speech at the Midland Bank, January 1924.

"Immense power and despotic economic domination are concentrated in the hands of a few. This power becomes particularly irresistible when exercised by those who, controlling money, govern credit and determine its granting. They supply, so to speak, the blood of the entire economic body, and withdraw it when it suits them: as if the soul of production were in their hands, so that no one dares to breathe against their will."

His Holiness Pius XI, "Quadragesimo Anno."

In the civilized world there are sufficient raw materials, labor, machinery, skilled labor, scientific and technological knowledge, and, in general, enough wealth to feed—indeed, to overfeed—its inhabitants. Nevertheless, in that civilized world there occur, regularly and cyclically, "economic" crises, worker unemployment, and their corollary: hunger. Orthodox economic science explains this phenomenon of cycles of prosperity and crisis by speaking of fictitious prosperity and overproduction, and reaches the bizarre conclusion that it is logical and natural for people to die of hunger and misery alongside overflowing stockpiles. Personally, I have come to the conclusion that so-called modern economic science represents a phenomenon similar to that of the painting that bearded "hippie" intellectuals call ultramodern and archaeologists call ancient. That is to say, it is a gigantic "bluff" that almost no one dares to denounce for fear of being seen as uninformed, backward, etc., in the eyes of the conformist masses who revere established ideas.

Because, whatever one may say, it is not natural—and therefore not possible—for people to die of hunger and misery because they have produced too many consumer goods.

The Spanish Penal Code—and, with it, all the penal codes of the world—punish counterfeiters with sentences that can reach life imprisonment. We dare to suppose that legislators do not impose such a drastic penalty to punish the counterfeiter who, by introducing his counterfeit bills into the market, obtains goods and services for them without working; but, above all, because by artificially increasing the money supply, he indirectly robs each and every one of his fellow citizens. The reason is simple: the more money there is, in a given situation, the less value it has. If a large-scale counterfeiting organization were to succeed, for example, in printing as many counterfeit bills as there are legal bills in circulation, every person would find that their money was worth exactly half of what it was worth before the counterfeiting organization in question began its activities. Counterfeiters are true thieves, since by releasing new currency—supposedly legal tender—into the market, they take for themselves a portion of the value of their fellow citizens' money, who are then forced to pay for the goods and services that these counterfeiters purchase.

In reality, any release of new money into the market—regardless of who does it—decreases the value of money in circulation. The owners of money in circulation prior to the release or issuance of new money suffer an obvious loss; and they realize this loss when they see that prices have risen and that, as a result, their money is worth less.

When does the issuance of new money occur? In the past, money was issued exclusively by governments, and its creation occurred as needs arose; since the function of money is simply to facilitate payment or the exchange of goods and services, the money supply was relatively stable in a given economic situation. Sometimes, the state would issue money, which was used to pay for public works and services, public education, state health institutions, public health, the military and police, civil servants, etc. With the state's creation of this new money, the public—the holders of money—suffered a loss in its value (remember that the more money there is in the market, the less value it has and the more prices rise), but that loss was offset, at least in large part, by the benefits directly or indirectly returned to the community through the public services and works carried out by the state.

That was in the past... because, nowadays, practically all states have relinquished their sovereign power to create or issue money in favor of individuals or private institutions that "legally" issue the vast majority of the money in circulation, to the point where it can be stated, without hyperbole, that no less than nine-tenths of the money currently in circulation in any given state is counterfeit money. If that description is too jarring, we can say that it is "abstract" money. With two aggravating factors: old-school counterfeiters had to be masterful imitators, verging on artists, and took great personal risks; modern counterfeiters create money with a simple stroke of the pen, with an entry in an accounting ledger, charge interest on such "money," and do all of this without any risk whatsoever; moreover, with the respect and distinguished regard of the flock of citizens destined to be annihilated.

Bankers were already operating in Europe in the early 17th century, before what is euphemistically called the "banking system" existed. Those who possessed gold and silver would hand it over for safekeeping to a banker, who would store it in a safe. The banker was nothing more than the guardian of his neighbors' savings, and, in exchange for the security he offered as custodian of others' gold and silver, he charged a small interest. The banker, naturally, gave his clients a receipt for their money. If a gentleman deposited a thousand gold reales in a bank safe, the banker would give him a receipt for a thousand reales. If the depositor later went to the bank to retrieve his money, the banker would return it (after deducting the legal interest of the time as guardian of the gold), and the receipt was destroyed. That receipt—an impeccable document upon which the greatest scam that the centuries have seen and will see was to be built—was, in reality, nothing more than an promise to pay, signed by the owner of a safe. These "promises to pay" were transferable and became, in fact, money. This was perfectly logical and convenient, since it was much more comfortable and feasible to use a piece of paper than to constantly carry bags of gold and silver around. These pieces of paper, these "promises to pay," were, in fact, used as money, based on the assumption that money is anything for which goods are delivered, services rendered, or debts paid.

Daily experience taught the bankers a curious fact. They realized that very rarely did their depositors return their receipts (their "promises to pay") in exchange for their gold. As a general rule—which has remained unchanged to this day—depositors withdrew, on average, ten percent of the total amount of their deposits. A man who deposited, for example, a thousand gold reales or any other legally accepted currency, such as silver, in a bank would withdraw, on average, a hundred reales for his living expenses and ordinary costs, and leave the remaining nine hundred in the bank. In other words, if a banker holding deposits worth one million reales lost, had stolen from, or spent nine hundred thousand, he still had the one hundred thousand necessary to meet the normal demands of his depositors.

Consequently, bankers began to put into circulation, multiplying them tenfold, more receipts, more "promises to pay" in gold than they actually possessed; that is, they lent out these "promises" and charged interest for doing so. One must not forget, even for a moment, that bankers lent—and continue to lend—something they do not possess, neither as owners nor as possessors; or, at most, in the latter capacity, ten percent of the total they "lent." Furthermore, as a guarantee of the owners' good faith, the bankers demanded, as collateral for their loans, the title deeds to the owners' houses, factories, farms, and crops; so that if a loan (increased by its accrued interest) was not repaid within a certain period, the banker would take possession of them.

Here is a digression. We draw attention to the fact that the banker did not, and does not, lend money, but simply a promise to pay it. The fact that goods and services were provided in exchange for such promises—that is, that they were used as money—did not in any way alter the fact that they were not money, but simply a promise to pay money and nothing more than that; with the aggravating factor that such promises lacked legal backing in gold and silver. Promises created "ex nihilo" (Editor's note: out of thin air) and yielding a hefty interest.

A loan has been defined as an exchange of debts. The lender—the banker—takes the collateral (title deeds to a house or factory, for example) and owes it to the borrower. The borrower, in turn, takes the "promises to pay," or the credit, as it is called, and owes that sum of money, plus interest, to the lender. In reality, what has occurred is an exchange of promises. The banker's promise to pay his client, in exchange for the client's promise to repay the money with interest. The client provides, as collateral, the title deeds to his house or factory. The banker gives nothing. It will be objected that the banker lends money and that this is his own guarantee. This is not true. The banker does not lend money; he has put into circulation "promises to pay money"—which is what he has actually lent—representing ten times more money than he has, and one who has ten cannot, nor will he ever be able to, lend a hundred. In other words, while banks hold against the community collateral representing real wealth—such as houses, factories, farms, crops, etc.—the community holds no collateral against the banks. The slightest attempt by a bank's creditors to enforce their "collateral" against it reveals that such collateral, in fact, has no substance whatsoever. If such creditors "put too much pressure" on the bank, they are punished by losing all their savings. The bank closes its doors, revealing that its "promises to pay" are false promises... unless the government comes to its aid with a moratorium... a moratorium whose consequences will ultimately mean that the community as a whole must pay to cover the banker's false promises.

But this is getting ahead of ourselves. Let us return to the period during which the banker is extending credit (his "promises to pay") to his fellow citizens. Suppose his depositors have deposited one hundred million pesetas in his bank. The banker has extended credit for one billion, handing out checkbooks to his customers. These checks, which will be used for future transactions, represent money created with a simple stroke of the pen in the bank's books; they play exactly the same role as counterfeit currency, since they increase purchasing power and, as a result, drive up prices and devalue the money that existed before the banker began his operations. In other words: by creating new money, the banker, just like a common counterfeiter, has stolen a little from each of his fellow citizens and has earned interest on the "money" stolen.

For now, the system seems to be working. The general euphoria masks the collective theft that has taken place. Borrowers have been able to generate new wealth, commerce is at its peak, and full employment has been achieved. Every time a loan is repaid—with its accumulated interest—the bank rushes to lend it out again. The billion units of "money" thrown into the market have caused the classic "boom." Prices are skyrocketing, while all kinds of products are offered for sale. But this rise in prices continues only as long as lending continues. Every time the banker stops making loans—that is, creating "money"—prices stop rising. And when prices stop rising, businesses collapse. The possibility of continuing to make more and greater profits in a bull market has vanished, because now the banker begins to find himself in trouble. In effect, he has lent out his "promises to pay"—or, if you will, has extended credit—for a billion pesetas. With the cash on hand, he has just enough to meet his customers' normal demands. Any extraordinary demand for funds could leave him overdrawn. Every credit line he has opened, represented by checks, as well as every receipt he has issued to his depositors, represents a promise to pay in gold and silver (today, tender paper currency issued by the state). Consequently, both his depositors and his borrowers—debtors and creditors—can demand gold and silver (or banknotes) in exchange for their receipts. Everyone is convinced that what the banker "lends" them is gold and silver (or banknotes issued by the state) and that checkbooks are used only for reasons of convenience and speed. But the banker knows, better than anyone, that this is not the case. He knows perfectly well that he has lent something he does not have, and that his peculiar business depends on the trust his clients place in him; that is, trust in the apparent interchangeability of metal and paper (today, of a check and the money it represents). His business is thus based on a breach of trust, on a fiction that must be maintained at all costs.

In the present situation, having created all the "promises to pay" that his reserves can cover—that is, ten times their total amount—the banker must refuse new loans. The market resists this. Those who have bought goods in the hope of reselling them at a higher price, or those who have produced goods to sell them at high prices, in turn begin to find themselves in an uncomfortable situation. A new phenomenon adds to the difficult situation that is developing: while the banker "invented" more and more money—let us emphasize that money is anything that serves as a medium of exchange—and, consequently, prices were rising, money changed hands with ease. Both real money (banknotes or coins) and, above all, the banker's famous "promises to pay" (checks) quickly pass from the buyer to the seller, and from the seller to the bank, from which a portion is withdrawn again to pay wages, bills, etc. Suppose Bank X extends a ten-million-peseta line of credit to Mr. Pérez, who hastens to use it to set up a factory and begins to launch products into a booming market. Mr. Pérez pays, by check, the builder, the blacksmith, the tinsmith, and the carpenter who have set up his factory. These specialists, in turn, have a checking account at Bank X, into which they deposit the checks in question. A portion of the value represented by those checks has been withdrawn to pay the wages of the workers employed by the builder, the carpenter, the tinsmith, etc. That money has been spent at local businesses: the supermarket, the butcher shop, the clothing store, etc., and these retailers have rushed to deposit it into their accounts at Bank X, where it remains until it is later withdrawn to pay their creditors (their suppliers): farmers, millers, textile manufacturers, etc. All these people are opening checking accounts at Bank X, and all these accounts are, in reality, nothing more than a simple statement of the value of the checks in the account holder's possession. The management of Bank X knows perfectly well that the checks totaling ten million that were lent to Mr. Pérez have been spent by him to pay the builder, the boilermaker, the carpenter, and the blacksmith. These gentlemen's accounts show positive balances, but what they actually possess are the checks from Bank X itself, which the bank had lent to Mr. Pérez.

Now, let's imagine that the general drop in prices alarms these gentlemen, who one fine day show up at the Payments window and demand to be paid in cash—but in real, genuine cash, in official banknotes issued by the government. And let's suppose that panic spreads, and just as has happened thousands of times throughout the history of banking, an army of customers shows up at the bank with identical demands...

Upon making these considerations—as simple as they are inevitable—the banker realizes that it is not enough to simply stop lending; he must begin to pressure his borrowers to get their accounts up to date. The management of Bank X calls Mr. Pérez and asks him to repay all, or a substantial portion, of the loan he received. Mr. Pérez, by pressuring his debtors—or selling off his inventory at a loss—manages to obtain the money needed to repay the bank loan. His debtors (customers, retailers, wholesalers, etc.) go to the bank and withdraw their money—in the form of checks—and use it to pay Mr. Pérez, who repays his loan to Bank X, which wipes out its "promissory notes" with a single stroke of the pen in its books.

Mr. Frederick Soddy, an English economist and 1921 Nobel Prize winner, wrote in his work *Citadel of Chaos*:

> "The most sinister and antisocial feature of book money is that it has no existence. Banks owe the public a total amount of money that does not exist. By buying and selling through checks, there is only a change in the particular person to whom the money is owed by the bank. While one customer's account is debited, another's is credited, and banks can continue to owe that amount indefinitely.

> The profit from issuing money has built the capital of the great banking business as it exists today. Having started with nothing of their own, bankers have put the whole world into indebtedness to them, irrevocably, through a trap.
>
> This money is created every time banks "lend" and disappears every time the loan is repaid to them. So if industry tries to pay, the nation's money disappears. This is what makes prosperity so dangerous, as it destroys money precisely when it is most needed, and precipitates a crisis."

It is evident that, when the banker began to extend his loans and, consequently, drove up prices, every buyer was in fact forced to pay him a kind of tribute; but when he contracted his loans again, thereby causing prices to fall, it was the sellers who had to pay him tribute. It is a classic case of "heads I win, tails you lose."[1] It is also a case of flagrant immorality, stemming from the fact that a man who began his activities with other people's money became, through the manipulation of "abstract money," the largest owner of estates, factories, land, and money… but concrete, authentic money—of the entire city and, in the long run, of the entire country.

Under the current banking system, bankers can use their checks to provide "purchasing power" to their fellow citizens, and then take it away at the very moment they need it most. The sudden flooding of a market with "abstract" money—true inflation—drives up prices and sparks widespread interest in increasing production. Markets become flooded with all kinds of products, and consequently, a great deal of money is needed to distribute them. (It is extremely important to bear in mind that the sole function of money is this: to distribute goods and services.) The sudden withdrawal of money, under such circumstances, necessarily causes a general fall in prices and, at the same time, a flood of bankruptcies... as well as unemployment and hunger.

This system, which will be the laughingstock of future generations, gives the banker control over the price level and, as a logical consequence, over wages. The banker has, practically, absolute power over his fellow citizens; a power that even the most tyrannical autocrat

---

[1] R. McNair Wilson. "*Promise to Pay,*" Omnia Veritas Ltd, www.omnia-veritas.com

could never have imagined. The power to subject anyone who dares to oppose them to their demands, through the latent threat of ruin. The modern banker—or, more accurately, the financial system—is in a position to ruin its debtors and "legally" seize their property. A. N. Field gives the following example:

"Suppose I am a banker and I lend a thousand dollars to John Smith, secured by his factory. I then call in a portion of my other loans, thereby reducing purchasing power in the region where John Smith conducts his business. As a result of this contraction in purchasing power, or 'demand,' prices will fall and John Smith will stop making money. Since he must pay me interest on my loan, he begins to lay off staff and install machinery that saves on labor. But I continue to reduce my loans. Prices continue to fall, and eventually, John Smith runs out of funds. He tells me he can no longer pay me the interest. So I seize the factory and put it up for sale. The best offer is eight hundred dollars, so I keep it as payment for my loan. A little later, I start lending again, and prices rise once more. John Smith's factory is now worth a great deal, for I have once again increased—by providing purchasing power—the so-called "demand" for what he manufactured. So I sell his business for five thousand dollars and pocket, "entirely legally," four thousand.[2]

This example might be called an exaggeration. In reality, every example, to be instructive, must be a caricature; to think is to exaggerate, Goethe said. But it illustrates a fact that has occurred many times in practice. Thus, in 1930, the United States of America had its warehouses full, but lacked the adequate amount of money to be able to conduct trade—that is, to get those products to consumers. Bankers had deliberately withdrawn eighteen billion dollars from circulation by refusing loans to prosperous farmers, merchants, and industrialists, and by calling in most of the existing ones. The famous "Black Friday" crash occurred, thousands of companies went bankrupt, and thirty percent of workers lost their jobs[3]. There was a surplus of goods, the

---

[2] A. N. Field. *"The Truth about the Slump."*

[3] On May 16, 1963, the Criminal Court of Nivelles (Belgium) heard the bankruptcy case involving the firm SOCOGA. Mr. Paul Marie de Launoy made the following statement before the judge: "The Banque Belge d'Afrique, of which I was the managing director of the Board, granted a loan of 61 million Belgian francs to SOCOGA." The President: "That is a lot for a bank with a capital of 100 million." The witness: "Of 144 million...and the bank had at that time 1,350 million francs in outstanding loans of all kinds." Later, the witness added: "Any entrepreneur can be on the verge of bankruptcy

granaries were overflowing—crops even had to be burned—labor—both skilled and unskilled—was available for work, but there was a lack of "money." The banks took possession of tens of thousands of industries, businesses, and farms. There was a lack of money... a lack of something that, while difficult to earn, is, on the other hand, the easiest thing to "make"... all that is needed is the government printing press, which backs and controls the amount issued, so that it is in proportion to the REAL wealth produced... Nevertheless, the U.S. government did not print the necessary money.

Why?... Because it could not, legally, do so. Since seventeen years earlier, in 1913, the government of the time had allowed, through a parliamentary fraud, the power to issue the country's currency to be wrested from it. Not just credit money, but legal tender.

The U.S. Constitution placed in the hands of Congress the right to create and control the country's currency. But in December 1913— —with most members of Congress spending their Christmas holidays at home, a law known as the "Federal Reserve Act" was passed almost surreptitiously. Broadly speaking, this law authorized the establishment of a Federal Reserve Corporation, with a Board of Directors (the "Federal Reserve Board"). This law stripped Congress of the right to create and control money, and granted it to the "Federal Reserve Corporation." The pretext given for the passage of this unusual law was "separating politics and money." The reality was that—in a great democracy often presented as the ideal prototype of that form of government—the power to create and control money was wrested from the so-called "representatives" of the people and granted to "A PRIVATE CORPORATION." And we do not believe we are committing the sin of rash judgment if we say that a private company will, by definition, tend to seek its own profit, whether or not this coincides with the general interest of the nation.

The most serious aspect of the 1913 Federal Reserve Act, from a legal standpoint, is that the decision was made by a minority of representatives, who, by all accounts, were pressured or bribed; the necessary quorum was not present...so that even from the strictest democratic standpoint, that law could not be justified...but the fact is

---

when his loans are withdrawn." Quoted in the newspaper "*Brisons le piège*," the organ of the Syndicom, 12 rue Henri Maubel, Brussels-10 (No. 1, June 1963).

that it was passed, and that since then, a private company has been issuing the currency of the most "democratic"—and powerful—country on the planet. Since that Christmas of 1913, a comparatively small number of people—some eight thousand—have controlled, issued, created, and destroyed at their convenience the money of the country that is supposed to be the standard-bearer of the West. The vast majority of these people are not even of American origin. The "deus ex machina" behind this disastrous "Act" was a banker from Hamburg named Paul M. Warburg.[4]

The "Federal Reserve Board" issues the country's money and then lends it to the "legal" government of the United States, at interest. If, for example, the government in Washington needs a billion dollars to finance public works, renew its arsenal, or whatever else, it must go to the "Board" and ask for that money. Then the all-powerful "Board" gives its approval on the condition that the government pay it interest. So Congress authorizes the Department of the Treasury to print one billion dollars in bonds, which are handed over to the Federal Reserve Board. The Federal Reserve Board pays the printing costs (which amount to about five hundred dollars) and makes the exchange. The government can then use the money to meet its needs.[5]

What are the results of this implausible transaction? Well, simply that the U.S. government has put its citizens in debt to the Federal Reserve Board for one billion dollars, plus interest, until it is paid off. The result of this insane financial policy (?) is that, in less than sixty years—from 1913 to the present—the people of the United States are in debt to the bankers of the Federal Reserve Board for a total of $350 million, with interest of one and a half trillion dollars each month, with no hope of ever being able to pay either the principal of the debt or even its interest, as both continue to rise. One hundred ninety-five million Americans are irrevocably indebted to some eight thousand other Americans; and the total amount of that debt exceeds the total value of

[4] A brother of this Warburg was implicated, and officially charged by the U.S. Secret Service, with having partially financed the Soviet revolutionaries of 1917. Another Warburg was stripped of his German citizenship as a result of the Reich's racial laws in 1933.

[5] Sheldon Emry. *"Billions for the Bankers. Debts for the People."*

all the country's wealth.[6]

There is more: Under this "debt-money" system, the bonds referred to above are converted into bank securities, on the basis of which banks can make loans to private customers. Since U.S. banking laws require only a 20 percent reserve, the banks of the "Federal Reserve Board" can make loans totaling up to five times the value of the bonds they hold[7]. That is to say, returning to the $1 billion transaction we used as an example, the right to interest on $6 billion... FOR AN ORIGINAL COST OF $500 in printing expenses.[8] And since Congress—in such a lofty Democracy—has abdicated the right to issue money, the only way left for industrialists, agricultural exploiters, and merchants in the United States to obtain money to develop the country's wealth is to "borrow" it from the Federal Reserve Banking Consortium and place themselves in its hands.

The terrible consequences of this insane "system" are glaringly obvious. Being omnipotent—and therefore irresponsible—the banks can wield the power of life and death over any company, no matter how strong it may be. The financial degeneration this entails leads to the grave extremes where, following the denial of a loan at a given moment, a company—no matter how strong—may be forced to sell its stock at any price—even at a pure loss—to meet its maturities and urgent obligations. After driving down the value of the merchandise, agents of the banking oligarchy buy up large quantities of the devalued stock; after this, the loan is approved, the stock rises in value, and is subsequently sold at fantastic profits. This practice of legalized theft has reached such a degree of sophistication today that the Federal Reserve Board need only announce in the newspapers a rise or a fall in its discount rate to cause the value of stocks to rise or fall as it wishes.[9]

Using these methods, the members of the "Federal Reserve" and their banking satellites have gained control of virtually all major American industries... and, from there, have begun their "coca-

---

[6] Sheldon Emry. Op. cit.

[7] James C. Oliver. "*A Treatise on Money*."

[8] Sheldon Emry. Op. cit. Eustace Clarence Mullins. "*On the Federal Reserve*," Omnia Veritas Ltd.

[9] Frederick Soddy. "*Citadel of Chaos*".

colonization" of the rest of the world.

To summarize, we will say that so-called "credit" consists of the bankers' false promise to pay out ten times more money than they have, derived from their depositors. Credit is not real, legal tender, but since it serves the same purpose—it is used to pay for goods and services and settle debts—it is, in fact, impossible to distinguish it from legal tender. These "promises to pay," issued by the banker via a checkbook, originate as "loans," which must be repaid with interest. Bankers reserve the "right" to withdraw their "promises"—their credit—and can thus, at their discretion, withdraw ninety percent of a country's purchasing power—the "demand." In fact, according to McNair[10], they are content with much smaller fluctuations, because "even very small fluctuations are sufficient to alter the price level in one direction or another"... alterations from which they profit.

None other than Sir Josiah Stamp, then the second-richest man in England and chairman of the British Railways, addressed 150 professors at the University of Texas in the following terms:

"The banking system was conceived in iniquity and born in sin. International bankers own the earth. Take away everything they have, but leave them the power to create[11] deposits, and with a few strokes of

[10] R. McNair Wilson. *"Promise to Pay,"* Omnia Veritas Ltd, www.omnia-veritas.com

[11] In the deliberately confusing banking terminology, the word "deposit" does not mean, as most people believe, the money deposited in the bank by a depositor. Bank deposits are, in fact, "loans of promises to pay legal tender," and often exceed customer deposits—shown on bank balance sheets as "Cash on Hand"—by as much as ten times. The term "Deposit," in banking terms in England, the United States, Australia, Canada, and New Zealand, means a loan. This is enshrined in the expression: "A loan creates a Deposit." So much so that scriptural money is called "Bank Deposit Money" in Anglo-Saxon countries. In Belgium, however, the word "Dépot" refers, in banking terms, to the money that depositors have actually deposited in banks for safekeeping and investment. The same is true in France. As for Spain, after consulting some bank balance sheets, the following is observed: 1: Sometimes the "Deposits" category is six times the size of the "Checking Accounts" category (during periods of crisis) and sometimes nine times the size (during periods of expansion). 2: Sometimes there is no correlation at all (undoubtedly because amounts corresponding to OTHER categories are included under one of these two headings, for the purpose of simplifying the financial reports in newspapers). 3: Sometimes the "Deposits" category represents, respectively, in periods of crisis or expansion, one-sixth or one-ninth of the "Checking Accounts" category. Linking the first and third observations, one reaches the logical conclusion that, puns aside, what banks lend—or, more precisely, intend to lend—

the pen they will create enough deposits to get it all back again. But if you take away their power to create money, all great fortunes will vanish, including mine, and this will be a much happier world. But if you wish to remain slaves to the banks and pay the costs of your own slavery, let them continue to create deposits"[12].

The incredibly ironic thing about this crystal-clear statement is that the man who made it, Sir Josiah Stamp, combined his role as chairman of "British Railways" with that of... Chairman of the Bank of England, an institution which, despite its official trappings, is, just like the "Federal Reserve Board," a private company that, since its founding, has almost always been run by individuals of the same background as those who have led and continue to lead the "Federal Reserve."

It is thus quite clear that the so-called economic crises are, in reality, financial crises, often deliberately and originating[13]. Thomas Jefferson once said: "I believe that banking institutions are more dangerous to our liberties than hostile armies." They have already succeeded in establishing a moneyed aristocracy that defies the government. The power to issue currency should be taken from them (Jefferson was referring, of course, to credit money) and returned to the people to whom it truly belongs."

In reality, the power to create money—both cash and credit money—should be reserved for the state, which would put it into circulation as needs dictated.

We must put an end once and for all to the seemingly inevitable "prosperity-crisis" or "inflation-deflation," or "boom-slump" cycle, or whatever it may be called. This fateful cycle has, for a country's economy, the same effects as a blood transfusion followed by a bloodletting just as the patient is beginning to recover. The main result of the "cycle" is the "prices-wages" race… in which the former always

---

represents six to nine times the total sum of what they hold.

[12] Quoted in "*Common Sense*," New Jersey, April 1, 1970.

[13] Under the "Federal Reserve Act," panics are artificially created, with the rigidity and precision of a mathematical problem, just as has just happened (1920). Charles Lindbergh, Sr.

win.

The circulation of currency in a given country should reflect exclusively its capacity to produce wealth, its potential for development, and the need for labor. Only the State—a sovereign and free State—whose officials have not had to "buy" the votes of their constituents with costly propaganda financed by those who control them… because he who pays the piper calls the tune. A State free from the gelatinous, invisible, omnipresent influence of Money Power can carry out a sound economic policy, free from the chains of "debt-money" and usury. Banks have an economic and social function to fulfill; in return for that function, they are entitled to fair and normal profits, but a nation's economy cannot be allowed to depend on banks; banks must serve the country, and not the country serve the banks.

The state must be not only the issuer of legal tender but also the provider of credit. Interest-free loans to solvent companies were the "deus ex machina" behind the colossal leap made by the German economy from 1933 to 1939; it was not, as has been absurdly claimed, the German people's great capacity for work. That work ethic—which is unquestionable—was not invented by the National Socialist regime, but its decision to wrest the power to "create" it from the banks was, without a doubt, the essential reason. One might object that states can make mistakes, can commit abuses, whatever their political color—red, white, or blue—whether or not their leaders attend Mass... but what no one can dispute is that while a state MAY make mistakes or MAY act against the common good in financial matters, a bank—or, even more so, a banking system—MUST necessarily act against that common good. And this is by definition: A state is a public institution and its function is the public good; a bank is a private enterprise and its function is its own private good, and it is natural that this should be so. What is not natural is that, through a centuries-old scam, the public function of facilitating and enabling the exchange of goods—such as the issuance of money (tender or credit)—has become a fabulous and immoral private monopoly.

It is unquestionable that if the primary obligation of a state is to protect its subjects—and, in the matter at hand, to protect them against debt-money and financial usury—the first measure that state must adopt must be to free itself from the control of what is commonly called

"Money Power." Juan Beneyto states[14] that "the entire enormous problem that the issue of Public Debt has posed for the state economy is related to the false construct of the state's need for money. The idea stems from the notion that the state should act like a private individual. The state must not act like a private individual. The state has three options to meet its financial needs: 1. Sovereignty over public services. 2. Sovereignty over the currency. 3. Sovereignty over finance. We must start from the distinction between the public and the private, because otherwise...the only path left is that of state indebtedness. The cure can only come through a state, such as the National Socialist state, that is master of the money. Only in this way is a strong state finance viable."

A debt-free state does not have to brutally tax its subjects to pay them off, as is currently the case in the United States. Germany from 1933 to 1939 was one of the countries with the lowest tax burden, and "the ultimate goal of our state," said Gottfried Feder, "is the establishment of a tax-free state"[15], citing as an example the State of Bavaria—which is not exactly one of the wealthiest in Germany—whose state treasury was built without a single pfenning of tax revenue. What Bavaria earned from the exploitation of state forests and gardens, railways, and postal and telegraph services offset its expenditures on cultural and educational services, public utilities, and the administration of justice. All tax revenue was allocated entirely to paying off the Bavarian debt and the corresponding portion of the national debt.

The state—whatever its political persuasion—is, by nature, a poor businessman. Hence the resounding failure of Marxism. The state's function is not to engage in commerce, but—in the realm of its domestic policy—to maintain public order, foster prosperity, and prevent abuses. In particular, we are opposed to the nationalization of companies, and, consequently, also to the nationalization of banking—a "solution" that would solve nothing and turn the state into a money trader when—as we hope to have already demonstrated—money is not a commodity, but a medium of exchange, and the catastrophe of "economic cycles" originates precisely in the artificial alteration of the value of something that should be fundamentally stable. When we say that Credit must be reserved for the State, we wish to emphasize—we repeat—that such

---

[14] Juan Beneyto, "*National Socialism.*" Quoting Gottfried Feder.

[15] Juan Beneyto. Op. cit. Ibid. Id.

credit must be interest-free. Plato already described the attempt to make money produce money as an "aberration against Nature."

And to put into practice the necessary, indispensable financial reform—which is the only alternative to the catastrophe of the "cycles"—all states need to do is enforce their Penal Code, which punishes the crime of counterfeiting currency, for that and nothing else is "credit-money" and "debt-money."

Either this, or the indefinite perpetuation of the Theft of the Centuries.

THE CENTURY OF THEFT

"There are two histories: the official, deceitful history, taught 'ad usum Delphini'; and the secret history, in which the true causes of events are found: a shameful history."

Honoré de Balzac

"Capitalism resembles Property as sophistry resembles reasoning, as Cain, perhaps, resembled Abel."

Edouard Drumont

Banking, which attained decisive power in the 19th century, has now reached absolute dominance over economic life, both in the "free enterprise" West and in the "communist" East. Today, when the launch of any enterprise is considered, whether for-profit or not, the first thing weighed is the likely attitude of the banking sector—local or national, depending on the nature of its activities—toward the enterprise in question. Nowadays, almost nothing can be done, and practically nothing can endure without the support of the banks. From mere executives of a service intended to facilitate the exchange of goods, bankers have successively become regulators; then controllers; and, finally, practically the masters of all the world's wealth. And, relying on that wealth, of political power.

Shylock and his medieval counterparts were innocent altar boys compared to the wizards of modern finance. After all, the moneylenders of that era charged as much as thirty to forty percent monthly interest... but one must not forget that this exorbitant interest, however abusive it may have been, was charged on existing, real, tangible money belonging to the usurer, who also ran immense personal risks, often resulting in prison sentences, if not "pogroms," expropriations, and expulsions. In contrast, modern bankers engage, broadly speaking, in the following operation: they borrow money—that of their depositors—for which they pay 0.5 percent interest. They then lend that money out at 9 percent, which represents a profit of 1,800 per cent; a profit that no business has ever yielded or will ever yield. It is astonishing to note how no government, no judge, no commission—such as the Tax Prosecutor's Office that existed years ago in Spain—has ever taken action against these money merchants—and monopolistic merchants, let us not forget—for abusive profits, when businesses have sometimes been shut down and their owners sent to prison for a mere 30 percent. But the banking abuse does not end here: banks do not earn "only" 1,800 percent, but rather, as we have already seen[16], by multiplying their loans by nine—creating scriptural money, or "fake money," as we will never tire of repeating—their profits, upon committing this genuine crime against the Penal Code and against humanity, are likewise multiplied by nine. For every hundred denarii[17] received from its depositors, the bank pays them an annual interest of half a denarius, and charges, when "lending" nine hundred denarii, an interest of 9 percent—that is, 81 denarii—which amounts to a profit of 16,200 percent[18]. And the heavens do not fall!

...Meanwhile, the cold-hearted state monsters prey on small and medium-sized business owners who hide their profits just to survive. And the bishops, tape measure in hand, measure the length of miniskirts, after which they laboriously produce a learned text in Latin... and all the holders of Power—of "official" Power, at least—maintain a deafening silence in the face of this secular outrage against humanity.

* * *

In "The Robbery of the Centuries" we have outlined, very briefly, a scheme of the activities of the "national" banker; of the man, or the banking institution, who "invents" non-existent money, from which he extracts interest that he makes his fellow citizens pay. Let us now

---

[16] In the first part titled "*The Robbery of the* Centuries" and written in 1971.

[17] We have avoided mentioning current currencies for two reasons: first, because the gentlemen of finance, as grotesque as it may seem, often take legal action against their critics on patriotic grounds; for example, there are those who equate the health of the dollar with "Christian-Western" civilization. The second reason—the one that has led us to favor the denarius—is based on the fact that this currency unit was used to pay for the services of the distinguished financier, Mr. Iscariot (Don Judas), for whom a statue has been erected in Moscow, and another in the Bronx, New York, the capital of International Finance.

[18] After deducting management and personnel expenses, etc., that percentage must be lower, but considering other operations in which banking trickery reaches great heights, it is not unreasonable to assume that this unprecedented deal yields a 20,000 percent profit.

observe another aspect of banking activities. What we might call the "international" banker lends his money (in reality, as we know, he neither lends nor owns the money) to firms engaged in trade with foreign countries. It is primarily in this banker's interest that the volume of foreign trade remain at a high level, in order to preserve the urgent demand for his "loans." It has not escaped his notice that when his colleagues, the "domestic" bankers, grant too many loans, the volume of exports tends to decline, since people can buy the goods produced in the country and export only what they have left over. In that case, the "international" banker has an interest in the "domestic" bankers reducing their loans. In reality, he does the same as the "national" banker: he grants loans—for amounts that are approximately nine times the total deposits of his checking account holders—to shipping companies, insurance companies, international transport firms, export firms, etc.

It was only natural, in keeping with the nature of things, that the "domestic" and "international" bankers would come to cooperate fully and completely, since their operations are governed by the same modus operandi and, moreover, complement each other admirably. Consequently, when, in banking jargon, a "boom" occurs in the domestic market, the "domestic" banker receives the support, the "credit," from his "international" colleague. And when this "prosperity" is followed by the inevitable, the cyclical "crisis," the "domestic" banker, having called in his loans, reopens them in favor of his colleague who finances exports, very often at rock-bottom prices, and even supported by state subsidies, to find a market for production that no one can buy in the country itself—because people have run out of means of payment—but which must be "placed" somewhere, if only to provide work for laborers and employees and avoid social chaos. In fact, "national" and "international" bankers have come to be completely indistinguishable, both personally and in terms of their activities.

* * *

The intricacies of the banking business lie in achieving a flexible price level, which logically results in a flexible wage level.

If a state were sufficiently strong and sufficiently just—, these two attributes must be complementary in politics—to set, to impose, a stable level of prices and wages, industrialists, farmers, merchants, etc., would be able to know, would be able to foresee in the long term what they would earn from their products. They could conduct their businesses rationally, and very soon they would be able to do without bank "loans," thus escaping the clutches of Debt. Bankers would not know what to do with their "loans." Their classic defeatist weapon—consisting of driving down prices through the sudden withdrawal of credit—would be rendered ineffective by government intervention, which, through the appropriate creation of new legal tender, would immediately raise prices back to their previous level. And if the banks went too far in creating credit, and prices consequently rose, the government would intervene again and, by applying, for example, taxes on non-essential goods and activities, or by issuing government bonds to finance public works, withdraw money from the markets, and prices would stabilize once more. Stability—the longed-for stability that all current governments seek without achieving it because they do not know how—or do not want—to tackle the problem head-on—would be achieved. Producers could have confidence in their markets, and the only thing they would need to worry about to survive would be noble competition in quality and, if anything, shifts in popular tastes and preferences. All competitive products would thus escape the banking yoke and acquire their own capital. Bankers would return to their original role as guardians of the public's savings, and for this custodial work, plus the provision of other services—including cooperation with the state in financing public works that are not immediately profitable—they would charge reasonable fees.

Adherents of liberal orthodoxy have always been fierce opponents of state intervention in price stabilization. The argument they put forward most forcefully is that freezing prices and wages has a disastrous effect on exports. The ideal of these gentlemen is for the so-called balance of payments to be favorable, that is, for exports to exceed imports. The curious thing is that they do not seem to realize that this cannot happen in all countries at the same time, since for every country with a favorable balance there must be, in theory—and in practice—another with an unfavorable balance. The logical consequence is economic war... and, following that, the other one. Total war. It is surprising to see how, in the realm of economics and finance, the musings of outdated liberals—generally pacifists, "," and sometimes well-intentioned people—lead, just as they do in the political arena, to war.

In reality, the purpose of economics is to meet the country's needs. That of finance is to rationalize the exchange of goods. If we were to follow the liberals in their argument that the currency loses value relative to foreign currencies due to the balance of payments deficit, we could rely on their own reasoning and tell them that if a country must live solely to send its products abroad, its currency—precisely because it has little value—should help it export. If half a denarius in foreign currency is worth, in a given country, one denarius, there is no doubt that that country can sell its products more cheaply abroad. But, in reality, we have no interest in kicking open the floodgates to the arguments of outdated Liberal Economics, because we categorically refuse to believe, as the die-hard export fanatics claim, that a country exists solely to send its products to foreign markets. What matters to a natural and healthy economy is the creation of a domestic market capable of purchasing domestic products. And when there is an excess of production of certain goods, they are sold abroad. This surplus is used to pay for the foreign products that are needed. Of course, the implementation of this system—which, incidentally, Germany followed with remarkable success between 1933 and 1939—means the end of the eccentricities[19], but, on the other hand, it also means the mobilization of all the country's productive activities in favor of creating a powerful domestic market; that industrialists buy from farmers and farmers from industrialists. And it signifies the restoration of agriculture as the most important of all industries[20].

* * *

The basic fallacy of International Finance could be expressed, parodying the generous and lyrical style of its spokespeople, as follows: "We must consider the Planet as a single unit. All men are brothers. Tribes were absorbed by kingdoms; kingdoms by empires. Now we

---

[19] Nothing is more original, in fact, than certain manifestations of the economic liberalism currently in vogue. French firms sell French wines to Belgium, and other French firms buy German—and French—wines from Belgium. Spanish firms buy plastics from Germany, and other—or the same—firms sell plastics to other countries, including Germany. Swedish firms sell umbrellas and coffins to Mauritania, and Spanish firms buy, in England, fabrics... that are Spanish.

[20] The most important does not necessarily mean the largest. It simply means the bond between people and their native soil, and this can only be achieved with a healthy and dignified rural population that is no longer the poor relation of human societies. If throughout Europe there were a peasantry of such high caliber as that of Normandy or Bavaria, or the admirable English "gentry," the future of our European homeland would inspire no fear in us.

have that marvelous creation of Human Reason: the UN. Yes, as all religions assure us, we are brothers, but that does not mean we cease to be partners in the 'Brave New World' enterprise. Only Finance can achieve that Brave New World. Money, and only Money, can guarantee a just and free distribution of wealth. Suppose borders were to disappear: economists would decide where to grow, for example, wheat or cotton. Not anarchy, as the selfishness of nationalism has allowed, but rationally, wherever it is quickest and cheapest. Next to the coal mines we would set up large industries; next to the iron mines, the foundries, and, right beside them—so as not to waste time and drive up the cost of goods—the exquisite settlements of our fellow workers, with large apartment buildings... very tall buildings, to lower the cost of land... and all identical.

Wouldn't that be wonderful? Wouldn't this splendid collaboration be a benefit to all? Wouldn't that put an end to the selfish and backward barriers of nationalism? What a wonderful vision! The entire Earth, developed and exploited rationally for the benefit of each of us, the partners in that great and generous enterprise! What stands in the way of the realization of this Edenic dream? Nationalism! What is nationalism? An outdated sentiment, consisting of thinking only of oneself and of people who resemble one; of despising foreigners, because they do not speak like us or are of a different color. Only Finance can carry out the magnanimous undertaking of putting an end to particularisms and creating the Great Society of Universal Consumption."

The reality, however, differs greatly from that idyllic picture... assuming it were idyllic, which for us is far from the case. The fact is that international finance is one of the causes of wars. International bankers extend credit in such a way that gold is rarely demanded by their borrowers. But if the balance of payments becomes heavily in deficit, or simply becomes too unbalanced, then a situation arises in which it is likely th, these borrowers will demand the gold—or the legal tender—that the bankers have promised to pay them, a promise for which they are paying interest in advance. "In the case of a country whose exports do not offset its imports, gold must be sent abroad to offset the unfavorable balance, because if this is not done, the country's currency will lose value relative to the currency of the country with which it trades"[21]. In other words, when a country's exports are exceeded by its imports, the value of its currency will tend to fall relative to others, for the simple reason that there will be more people using it to buy foreign currencies than people using foreign currencies to buy the currency of the country in question. The only way to prevent the currency from losing value is by exporting gold. But since international bankers—like their domestic counterparts—have issued "promises to pay" (loans) amounting to nine times more money than they actually possess, it is clear that they must impose very strict limits on gold exports[22], for if this demand for gold persists even slightly longer than normal, the bankers will be forced to declare bankruptcy and close their doors. How can they protect themselves? By refusing new loans and forcing their clients to settle, or at least reduce, their outstanding debts. In other words, they act like their colleagues, the domestic bankers. The result is that a large quantity of goods intended for export floods the domestic market, prices plummet, and panic ensues. To prevent this panic, there is no choice but to lower the prices of goods for export—often with state subsidies—which represents an additional blow not only to the economy but also to the country's morale, as it has had to subordinate the purchasing power of its currency to the interests of international bankers. In order to ensure that products intended for export are as low-cost as possible, the wages of workers and employees are sacrificed, quality is compromised, and commercial practices are employed that are increasingly at odds with ethics and the most basic decency. And in the age of mechanization and overproduction, poverty and overflowing stockpiles coexist; the classes blame one another; there are strikes and lockouts, and no one, or very few, realize who is the true cause of the disaster; they do not see that the modern alchemists of banking, with their "promises to pay" for what they do not have, enervate, demoralize, and ruin their victims—that is, all of Humanity. The root of all "economic" evils is none other than the granting of credit by banking institutions— —that do not possess the money necessary to honor their "promises to pay." All the world's bankers, both national and international, are in the same situation: all of them have lent out, in "promises to pay," nine times more fiat money than they actually have in custody; and all of them also live in constant fear that sudden demands will arise for the redemption of their "promises" in an amount exceeding their comparatively small reserves

[21] R. Mc Nair Wilson: "*Promise to pay,*" Omnia Veritas Ltd.

[22] R. Mc. Nair Wilson: Ibid. Id.

of real money. The gold standard—or any other standard—is nothing more than "a device invented to safeguard foreign exchange and, in this way, spare the banks from the onslaught of their creditors, which would reveal that the bankers are in a state of permanent insolvency"[23].

* * *

A necessarily very brief digression on the Gold Standard, which will undoubtedly be the laughingstock of times to come. Orthodox liberals and physiocrats claim that money, to perform its function effectively, must have intrinsic value. At first, the value of gold coins; later, the gold that was supposedly in the banker's vaults, and which he promised to pay upon delivery of the banknote (a genuine receipt), even though eight out of nine of that gentleman's promises were false. The financiers' apprehension regarding currency issuance by the state—labeled "inflation"—is well known, as if banking activities were not characterized, precisely, by an alternating cycle of inflation and deflation that squeezes the people. The reality is that the Gold Standard Gertrude Coogan[24] gives the following example to illustrate the fallacy of the gold standard: A government builds a theater with a capacity for a thousand spectators. But since, for some strange reason lost in the mists of time, it is believed that the tickets must be made of gold and the government lacks that metal, it turns to the only person in the country who happens to possess gold and commissions him to issue the tickets. This man soon realizes that people find it uncomfortable and cumbersome to carry

the heavy tickets in their pockets, and, out of pure charity, to spare his fellow citizens—future spectators of the government theater—any inconvenience, he provides them with small pieces of paper on which, in impeccable calligraphy, the following phrase is written: "I promise to pay the bearer a gold ticket." On opening night, barely a tenth of the theater's seats are occupied, though on the street, at the theater's entrance, many potential spectators would have liked to enter. When the Minister of Culture approached the issuer of the tickets to ask the reason for this anomaly and urged him to provide the necessary tickets to fill the theater, the issuer replied that this was not possible, as his

[23] Hermann Hoppker Aschoff. *"Money and Gold."*

[24] Gertrude M. Coogan. *"Money Creators."*

tickets were "receipts for gold tickets." What he did not say was that, in fact, he had already put nine or ten times as many receipts into circulation as there were actual gold tickets in his safe. He was afraid to issue more receipts, in case people suddenly, for some reason, began demanding the gold tickets instead of their paper receipts. Since he was determined to prevent the government from realizing that the theater could be filled with paper receipts, he began to wave the specter of inflation. "The value of the tickets lies in the fact that they are made of gold," asserted the ticket issuer-dealer. "The irresponsible politicians who seek to issue paper tickets are inflationists and enemies of the theater arts"... "No, sir," replied the Minister of Culture. "What we intend is to fill the theater, and for our fellow citizens to use the seats we have arranged for them. Inflation, if anything, would consist of issuing more than a thousand tickets. But as long as there are empty seats, why can't we continue issuing tickets?"... "Because they are tickets that cannot be exchanged for gold.

Would you enjoy a theatrical performance knowing that your ticket is nothing more than a worthless piece of paper?" insisted the impresario, who concluded with his decisive argument: "How can you be sure you won't print too many paper tickets, so that many ticket holders are forced to stay out on the street?" "Because we know the number of seats in the theater," replied the Minister.

Well, there is no doubt that any modern government is fully aware of a country's income—its wealth. With proper management of statistics and information technology, the risk of inflation is practically nonexistent. Moreover, assuming that, to cover up the mismanagement of state-run enterprises[25], the government allows to get carried away and overwork the Mint's printing presses, the resulting inflation will be insignificant compared to the colossal banking inflation.

* * *

We have outlined, in very broad strokes, the financial system. The root of that system is a lie. The lie of a man who, having promised to

---

[25] We insist that the ideal is for the State to devote itself to its specific mission, namely, the realization of the national Idea, the moral and physical (racial) protection of the People, and the preservation of order. For, to date, history provides not a single example of a merchant-state whose management was beneficial to the nation.

pay nine times more than he possesses, is supposed to be capable of fulfilling such a promise. From there, a cascade of further lies ensues: the lie that a loss of gold is a national disaster; the lie that foreign exchange rates must remain fixed; the lie that prices and wages "cannot" be stabilized; the lie that a country lives solely on its exports; the lie that the domestic market must be subordinate to the foreign market; the lie that high wages are a danger; the lie that a country that imports more than it exports "lives beyond its means," and the lie that the remedy for overproduction is the burning of crops to safeguard prices.

And, alongside that pyramid of lies, the spectacle of technological progress, with overflowing stockpiles that cannot be distributed...for the sole reason that, against all odds, it is necessary to maintain the Empire of Lies.

Whether we like it or not, we must acknowledge the fact that, in our time, there is a close interdependence between Money and Power. Since finance is, by its very nature, international, the power it seeks is equally international. The globalists, the apologists for the UN, are financiers or act on behalf of the financial establishment. The world is governed today, both politically and economically, by certain men serving certain Forces, which in North America are known as the "Establishment." These men occupy key positions, although it is not essential that their official political rank be preeminent. Thus, for example, it is curious to note how the Presidents of the United States, elected by universal suffrage, seem incapable of making any decision without first consulting a sort of "viziers," handpicked for the role. Nixon has Kissinger, who comes from the powerful Goldman, Sachs & Co. banking firm, just as Johnson and Eisenhower had Sidney Weinberg, from the same banking institution and at the same time closely linked to the Rockefellers; and Kennedy, Truman, and Roosevelt had Bernard Mannes Baruch, advisor to 29 banks[26] and Felix Frankfurter, a man of the Warburgs, the "gods" of the Federal Reserve Board[27]. Did Nixon, Johnson, Kennedy, and Roosevelt have...? Or rather, did Kissinger,

---

[26] Dan Smoot, *"The Invisible Government."*

[27] Two curious circumstances converge in all these gentlemen: they come from Germany, and by their appearance, they must be descendants of the Teutonic Knights of the Hanseatic Order.

Weinberg, Frankfurter, or Baruch have them?

Who had whom?...To answer this dilemma, it suffices to recall Céline's phrase: "Democracy is plutocracy." Elections are always won by the candidate with the most money at their disposal to fund their campaign—an exorbitantly expensive circus that only the financial elite can sustain. And as we all know: he who pays the piper calls the tune. In England, when the Conservatives are in power (who are gentlemen who play at Labour politics), it is public knowledge that the "gray eminences" are Charles Clore and Jack Cotton, two super-financiers from the City of London; when the Labour Party is in power (who are shopkeepers making fools of themselves), another group of financiers appears surrounding Harold Wilson: Wolfson, Bernstein, Cohen, Zuckerman, and Maxwell—[28], all of them closely linked to the all-powerful Lazard Bank. Most political figures of any significance in France are also linked to the Lazards and the Rothschilds, whether they are labeled as left-wing, right-wing, or centrist.[29]

The global "Establishment" is made up of some three hundred families of ancient lineage, closely linked to one another by family and economic ties. It exercises virtually total control over the global advertising market, through which it subjugates the news market: press, radio, and television. The global wheat market is associated with the name Dreyfuss[30]. In the chemical industry, seven major consortia—among which the "Imperial Chemical Industries" trust stands out,, created by the Melchett (a) Mond (a) Moritz family—account for ninety percent of global production. The nickel market is a joint venture of the Mond and Rothschild families. The Rothschilds are also the world's leading power in the mercury market. The diamond, silver, gold, copper, and steel markets are associated with the names of Oppenheimer, Barnato, Beit, Goldschmidt, Guggenheim, Wernek, De

---

[28] After nourishing our spirit by contemplating the faces of these gentlemen in the London magazine "Spearhead," our doubts have been dispelled: they are pure specimens of the old Irish nobility, including Maxwell, who arrived in Great Britain in 1939 from Czechoslovakia, where—for reasons that biographers will no doubt one day clarify—he suddenly felt unsettled.

[29] The Rothschilds, originally from Frankfurt, are of Austrian nobility. Indeed, Kaiser Franz Joseph granted the barony to Nathan Rothschild.

[30] The Dreyfusses are originally from Lorraine, like Joan of Arc.

Wendel[31], Lewinsohn, Rothschild, Bleichroeder, Japhet, Seligman, Lazard, Morgenthau, Schiff, and Warburg[32]. The Zemurray family, owners of "United Fruit," controls half a dozen Central American republics and wields great influence in South America. The Gunzbourg family[33] has major interests in Japan, where it controls numerous industries. It would be tedious to list the complete roster of families that make up the "Establishment"; even a very brief description of their activities would require a volume dedicated exclusively to that purpose; we shall therefore leave it for a better occasion. It suffices for now to point out that, for the "Establishment," there are no borders or "iron curtains"...thus, for example, the Achberg family has controlled the Soviet State Bank since 1917. The Achbergs, of "Nya Banken" in Stockholm, are regarded as the agents of the Rothschild family in Northern Europe.

The "Establishment" rarely acts directly. The barons of high finance act through their trustees, who tightly control the administration. In France, for example, Henry Coston recounts that in this country of liberty, whose democratic motto is inscribed on the facades of public buildings, "all economic activities are closely controlled by the Administration; there is a dictator of credit: Mr. Bloch-Lainé; a dictator of agricultural policy: Mr. Rosenstock-Franck; a dictator of productivity: Mr. Ardant; and a dictator of the Development Plan: Mr. Étienne Hirsch"[34].

In three centuries, the wretched dregs of Europe have climbed to the pinnacle of world power. All that remains is the definitive consolidation of itself—that is, the synthesis of capitalism and communism—after which "Peace" will come. Peace without Justice, satanic peace. The peace of the human flock, with some three hundred shepherds and a few thousand police dogs. To reach the summit, a few men scattered across

---

[31] The De Wendels are not of ancient lineage, though they have considerable family ties—and above all, ties of interest—with the upper echelons of society.

[32] The Warburgs are at the top of the financial pyramid. Old "Junkers" from the Baltic.

[33] The Gunzburgs, along with the Warburgs, Schiffs, and Kahns, were financiers of the Glorious Red Revolution of October 1917 (Louis Marschalko, "*World Conquerors*," Omnia Veritas Ltd, www.omnia-veritas.com).

[34] All of them "knights" of Burgundy and descendants of Vercingetorix. The quote from Henry Coston comes from the work "*La Haute Banque et les trusts*."

the Old Continent and despised by Humanity conceived, some three hundred years ago, the greatest theft in History: the Theft of the Centuries. Today, in our "civilized" and "democratic" 20th century, their descendants, with full legal authority and, moreover, a reputation for respectability, reign secretly but despotically over the human race. It is the century of thefts.

THE CAPITALIST ENIGMA

The purpose of the machine is production, and that of production is consumption.
Currency is an instrument of measurement and exchange: not a commodity.
The Wealth of a Nation lies in the Labor and Culture of its inhabitants. (A truism, the Forgotten)

MISERY IN ABUNDANCE

The great paradox of the current economic crisis—which should really be called a financial crisis—is that people cannot acquire the goods they have actually produced. In other words, we could say that we find ourselves in a situation of poverty amidst overproduction. If this idea were to take firm root in people's minds, the decisive step toward solving the problem would have been taken. It would, in truth, the first step, the essential step, the one that demonstrates that all so-called "economic science" is nothing more than the pretentious and vacuous jumble of a swarm of clowns, called economists, subsidized most of the time—directly or indirectly, knowingly or, more often, unknowingly—by the beneficiaries of the insane situation the world is suffering.

It is abundantly clear that if the West has managed to produce goods and is in a position to provide services, both of which more than cover its current needs, it should be experiencing a period of well-being unparalleled in its entire history. Why do the goods produced find no buyers? The answer is obvious. Because consumers are not in a position to buy them. This situation can be scientifically explained by the fact that people's purchasing power has declined everywhere.

If anyone denies this impoverishment amidst abundance, let us observe some notable and illustrative facts. On the one hand, we see that in France and Italy, agriculture—which is the economic sector that has progressed the least in absolute terms—yields 35 percent more output than it did forty years ago[35]. In industry, relentless technical progress allows for greater production at an ever-increasing pace[36]. Despite strikes, wars, the loss of colonies, and social chaos, these two countries have—at the very least—doubled their industrial production over the last forty years. It would be closer to the truth to say they have tripled it, but there are practically no sources worthy of full credit due

[35] *Encyclopedia Britannica*. Britannica Book of the Year, 1967–68–69. Edited by William Benton. pp. 453, 452, 442.

[36] Italian electricity production increased by 15 percent in 1968 and by another 12 percent in 1969, which was a particularly "social" year (66 days of strikes). Ibid. Id. 1970, p. 429.

to the pollution of their waters with low politics in the most pejorative sense of the word. On the other hand, we see that the French population, during that same period, has barely increased by five percent, and the Italian population by nine percent. Simple arithmetic shows that these two countries should be experiencing an era of economic prosperity unprecedented in their entire history.

Furthermore, we observe that despite Italy being the country with the highest number of emigrants in all of Western Europe, there were, by mid-1976, more than one and a half million unemployed and nearly one million in France. The figure must have been exceeded in Spain as well, and this despite the absence of free dismissal and the fact that the manufacturing behemoths of the National Institute of Industry—deficit-ridden by definition, like every state-owned enterprise, from RENFE to the last Ukrainian kolkhoz—absorb a significant workforce, whose politically mandated wages will ultimately be paid, in the form of taxes, by the people.

That millions of workers across Europe, upon losing their jobs, are left without wages—or receive the pittance of unemployment benefits, which amounts to shifting the burden of the unemployed onto the entire nation—is a logical consequence of cause and effect. "The crisis is the cause of unemployment," some economists will exclaim, addressing the audience with great seriousness from one side of the ring. "No! You are wrong. Unemployment is the cause of the crisis," other economists will reply, with the seriousness of fine circus professionals. Tradition demands that clownish arguments end with cream pies being thrown at each other's heads, while young and old alike fill their lungs and release their healthy doses of adrenaline. Unfortunately, in the prosaic world of economics and finance, these academic debates are the prelude to tragically real and serious conflicts, in which the old production-consumption dilemma is easily overcome, as consumers consume the entire output in the form of shells.

ORGANIC ECONOMY

Economics is a way of thinking, just as morality, aesthetics, ethics, and politics are. Each of these forms of thought isolates a part of the totality of the world and claims it for itself. Morality distinguishes between good and evil; aesthetics between beauty and ugliness; economics between useful and useless, and, in its final, purely commercial phase, between profitable and unprofitable[37].

We have alluded to Politics, which divides men into friends and enemies. Considering the body politic as an organic whole, there is no doubt whatsoever that Economics is part of Politics. A part that is, in its entirety, subordinate to the political whole. Economics is to the political whole what the digestive system is to the entirety of an organic being[38] and yes, as one ascends the organic scale, from the plant to the human being, passing through the animal, the digestive system becomes relatively less important—we insist on this relativity—and such importance diminishes even further upon reaching the supreme organic being par excellence, the Great Culture. It is, then, among its constituent organs, an "ultimus inter pares," and its function, though vital, is the least noble of all. Having made this caveat, we consider it essential to emphasize the fact that just as an individual can die from intestinal paralysis, which in turn causes peritonitis, so too can a Great Culture—and, a fortiori, a nation—become seriously ill and even perish—disappear—due to the chaos created by an economic illness that is misdiagnosed and, consequently, inadequately treated. And we do not believe that the current spectacle of misery amidst abundance leaves any doubt regarding the fact of the Western economy's illness. An illness, moreover, that is degenerative, for it has spread from the digestive system throughout the entire body of the organism, including its brain, since something must be functioning poorly in the latter if it passively accepts situations that defy simple common sense, such as the deliberate destruction of crops to "maintain the course of agricultural

[37] Francis Parker Yockey: "*Imperium*," Omnia Veritas Ltd, www.omnia-veritas.com.

[38] J. Bochaca: "*Finance and Power,*" Omnia Veritas Ltd.

prices."

We have said that the economy is a part subordinate to the whol r political. A further example of the pathological nature of the current situation is provided by the fact that the opposite is taken as true—that is, that politics is subordinate to the economy, and that the economy is the engine of history—an absurdity propagated by Marx but, unusually, endorsed to varying degrees by his class enemies, the so-called "capitalists"... an apparent paradox we will address later.

SCOPE

Let us turn our attention to the economy of the entity known as Western Civilization—that is, Europe and its cultural colonies scattered throughout the world—in a word: the White World. We once stated[39] that "it is necessary to draw a distinction between the civilized world and the uncivilized, underdeveloped, or under-capable world, or whatever one may choose to call it." We added that for the underdeveloped, under present conditions and for many centuries to come, there was no solution to their economic problems, even with fabulous, untapped resources and the non-repayable aid provided by the United States, Europe, and globalist organizations—and, with an eye toward political influence, by the countries of the so-called Communist bloc. We reasoned this by arguing that the Economy was subordinate to Race—which we could describe as "the hallmarks of the political organism"—and we concluded that "an industrial or mining operation run by the English, Italians, Germans, or Swedes will likely succeed, whereas the same operation, run by Bantu, Mambara, or Nepalese, will be a total failure." We compounded our case—and we consider it our duty to reiterate it here and now—by asserting that the sight of a pariah starving to death before a sacred cow, or of any other Indian lying on fertile soil that is left uncultivated so as not to scratch Mother Earth and provoke the wrath of the gods, leaves us completely indifferent.

The reason for such indifference is twofold: first, because we share the outdated belief that before solving the problems of others, one must solve one's own, especially when people of color never miss an opportunity to remind us that they are now "independent"[40] and to blame us for all their miseries; second, because happiness cannot be exported. Happiness—that is, self-realization—is something absolutely

---

[39] CEDADE Bulletin No. 24. June–July 1970.

[40] Naturally, this is a purely formal independence. One need only have even a rudimentary understanding of the dynamics of power to realize that independence is a fact, not a right enshrined on parchment, even if such a "right" is recognized by all UN member states. Now President Bingobango of the Democratic Republic of Monomotapa listens to the advice of Abramovitch, the Soviet ambassador, or Abrahanson, the American ambassador.

personal, both at the level of the individual human being and that of a Superior Culture. What fully satisfies a European may leave a Japanese person unsatisfied, and vice versa. And we choose as an example the foreigner who is closest, despite differences in distance and status, to the Westerner. We have seen, in South Africa, Kaffirs with nose rings, driving gleaming "Mercedes," wearing impeccable European suits, and barefoot. These Kaffirs live in huts identical to those seen near the Kinshasa Airport (formerly Leopoldville), which in turn must be the same as those built by their ancestors a thousand years ago. Where the white man imposed, during the colonial era, churches, hospitals, and roads, sorcerers, magicians, and goat trails are quickly returning. Hygiene is second nature to Europeans: far less so to Asians; Arabs must be compelled, under the strictest religious precepts, to perform ablutions, and in Black neighborhoods and cities around the world, under diverse climates and circumstances, from Johannesburg to New York, and from Nairobi to King's Cross (Sydney, Australia), the filth is proverbial, with the supposed—and certainly false—poverty of Black people having no bearing on this whatsoever. Finally, instead of so many statistics on children of color who cannot eat as much as they would like, accompanied by grotesque and heart-wrenching photographs designed to provoke the directed compassion of the naive Aryan, it would be better if we were provided with a cold, objective study of what these beggar peoples have done since they "obtained"—let's put it that way—their sacred independence. For we find nothing more grotesque or more cynical than those campaigns to alleviate hunger in India, while that country's government announces with great fanfare in the world press that it now possesses the atomic bomb. And the weeping accountants of the Kremlin, of the countless socialist parties, and of the various positive religions—who are so concerned with calculating how many hospitals could be built in Black Africa and how many Asians could eat for six months with the money it cost for just one of the space projects— are wasting such an excellent opportunity to enlighten the peaceful Indian government on the number of outcasts who could be fed lavishly with the money their brand-new atomic bomb cost them.

STATEMENT OF THE PROBLEM

Within the context of our Western economy, the current crisis can be summarized as follows:

a).- In the civilized world, there are sufficient raw materials, skilled labor, unskilled labor, and scientific knowledge to abundantly satisfy the needs of its inhabitants.

b).- Poverty and scarcity exist because people do not have enough money to buy the goods produced by modern industry and agriculture at a price that is attractive to producers.

c).- When one lacks something, the most obvious remedy is to create it, and there is no physical difficulty in creating more money.

d).- Inflation, which occurs when there is more money than goods, is clearly a calamity; however, the gradual increase in both money and goods—such that the purchasing power of money remains on par with production and prices stay stable—has nothing to do with inflation and is, ultimately, what we need.

e).- Machinery and the use of natural resources increasingly limit the need for human labor, while increasing the production of wealth in goods and services. Consequently, people displaced from paid work by machinery must receive enough money to be able to purchase what is produced by the machines that have displaced them from their jobs. This money, of course, must not be taken from other people's pockets, even if done through the invisible means of taxes, for then all we will be doing is robbing some to pay others, and our society is already sufficiently developed that we have no need to play at being Dick Turpin; we must not allow the unemployed to be a burden on those who work, nor should we consider machines a curse when they should, on the contrary, be a blessing to humanity by freeing it from many hours of labor and allowing people to devote those hours to cultural activities or to leisure— r creative pursuits, such as gardening, sports, hiking, study, etc.

And that is all. This is the problem. That is the question. And if we wish to solve the problem posed in the five preceding points, which summarize the To Be or Not To Be of the Western Economy, we must ask ourselves, with Shakespeare, what is better for the spirit:

to suffer the slings and arrows of outrageous fortune, or to take up arms against a sea of troubles and by opposing end them? For the famous Hamletian soliloquy applies to the present Western situation, on the political plane—which, by definition, is all-encompassing—and therefore also on the economic plane. What should we do? Accept the explanation of classical economists who claim that cycles of prosperity and misery must follow one another by virtue of a mysterious economic law? Or, better yet, take up the arms of common sense to confront the sea of economic calamities that the Great Parasite has in store for us, and overcome them? To formulate the dilemma in this way is to resolve it. Let us, then, take up the weapons of common sense and stand up to it.

Almost everyone imagines that understanding our monetary system requires a gifted mind and a special talent for mathematics. Nothing could be further from the truth; it is engineering, not finance, that demands a mastery of advanced mathematics: to understand how modern finance works, all that is needed is to approach the problem without prejudice; to see things as they are, and not as we are told they should be; to use what the English call "common sense" and the French "bon sens"—which we could roughly translate into Spanish as "sentido común"—and to employ the old but ever-relevant philosophical method of the Thomist school, "reduction to the absurd," which consists of rejecting any conclusion, no matter how logical its premises may seem, if such a conclusion leads to an absurdity, such as, for example, that the whole is less than its parts, that two solids can occupy the same space at the same time... or that, as the soothsayers of modern economics claim, what must be done to protect agriculture is to burn its crops.

THE MACHINE

Until the mid-18th century, agriculture and industry relied primarily on the muscular power of horses and oxen, and on the muscular and mental power of man. But in early 1765, a Scotsman, James Watt, devised the steam engine, which was coupled to the mechanism of a cotton loom. The Industrial Revolution had just begun. The results of this revolution demonstrate beyond a shadow of a doubt that point a), which we mentioned in the previous section, is absolutely true, for indeed, in the civilized world there are sufficient raw materials to satisfy the needs of its inhabitants, and these raw materials have been developed and made available to man thanks to the aid of the machine.

A digression is necessary. In the aforementioned point a), apart from raw materials, other factors are involved, such as labor and scientific knowledge. We will discuss this later. For now, let us limit ourselves to the raw materials, developed by the machine.

Once set on the path to success, nothing could hold back the machine's progress. Science became its ally, and astonishing discoveries followed one after another—not only in the field of steam but also in hydraulic power, electricity, chemistry, new fuels (especially coal and oil), industrial gases, and so on. Then came the use of atomic energy, and around 1938 in Germany the first attempts began to harness the source of all power: solar energy—research that was interrupted by the war and has since regained momentum in France. Today, with just two centuries of inventions and development, the machine dominates the world. Its astonishing achievements have made man the Lord of the Earth, and in moving from an era of scarcity—before Watt—to one of abundance—after Watt—they have completely transformed the approach to economics, even as the high priests of this "science" cling to dogmas that were, perhaps, valid for times past—when a poor harvest due to drought or a locust plague would bring a country to the brink of collapse—but which are ridiculously outdated in our times.

We know that in 1935, in the countries of Europe (with the exception, of course, of Russia and Turkey), in the United States, Canada, New Zealand, and Australia, machinery had made available to mankind just over one billion horsepower[41]. Today, and despite the political and social sabotage to which it has been subjected, we have surpassed three billion[42] and yet atomic energy, radioactivity, solar energy, and tidal energy are still far from having had their final say.

The British Nobel laureate, Professor Soddy, calculated in 1935 that only 4,000 men, equipped with modern machinery—we repeat, machinery from forty years ago—could harvest the entire wheat crop of the United States[43]. Let us note that the United States is the world's second-largest potential wheat producer, but that thanks to the admirable socialist system implemented in Ukraine, it has risen to an undisputed first place and still allows itself the debatable political luxury of selling its wheat surpluses to the USSR—whose production is barely greater than that of Western Europe—at low prices and on credit terms.

An Australian incubator, with a capacity of 1,100,000 eggs, hatches 6,600,000 chicks a year using electricity[44]. The phylloxera plague, which in 1846 ruined the potato harvest in Silesia and the Palatinate, can now be eliminated by two planes equipped with poison gas in a couple of hours at most[45].

The British, in 1925, and the Germans, in 1934, discovered separate systems for the manufacture of synthetic nitrates, which, apart from being much cheaper than natural ones—which in any case were insufficient for our needs and had to be sourced from Chile—yielded significantly higher returns.

In 1933, a machine for manufacturing light bulbs was invented in Germany, allowing the well-known firm Osram to supply the entire market in just a few weeks[46].

---

[41] Frederick Soddy: "*Citadel of Chaos,*" p. 88.

[42] Britannica Book of the Year 1969, pp. 356–362.

[43] Frederick Soddy: "*Citadel of Chaos,*" p. 93.

[44] Stuart Chase: "*Men and Machines,*" p. 47.

[45] Maurice Colbourne: "*Economic Nationalism,*" p. 49.

[46] Maurice Colbourne: "*The New Economy,*" p. 47.

The English author Colbourne cites a telling example which, we note, refers to the year... 1930! : "The world population in 1930 was about 2 billion people. In the same year (according to Mr. Donald Ferguson of the Statistics Department of the British Association of Electricity and Manufactures) 'the total capacity of machinery was 390 million horsepower' (this figure excludes automobiles). Thus, the world, apart from its automobiles, had machinery equivalent to 3.9 billion strong men. That is to say, for every consuming unit there are two non-consuming units"[47]. We repeat, these data refer to the year 1930, but, as we have already seen, in 1939, that is, just nine years later, in the White World—which then accounted for four-fifths of the world's industrial power[48] —the figure had reached one billion horsepower, which, for a population of some six hundred million people, meant that for every consuming unit there were, on the eve of World War II, sixteen non-consuming units in the Western World. Under such conditions, to claim—as the economist-buddhas, devotees of the god Marx, have done with sophistical cynicism—that the Great War broke out for economic reasons is something that should prompt the circus artists' union to sue said economists for professional intrusion and unfair competition. Now, if they were to replace the word "economic" with "financial," they would already be on the path to Truth, but such Buddhas know full well that said path is barred to them.

Economic problems in the West, when Ford factories in the United States build, on average, one car every four seconds? Economic problems when Bayer factories in Germany can supply, also on average, their rich domestic market in two months and devote the rest of the time to working for foreign markets? Economic problems when West German agriculture produces the same as in the real Germany—that of 1939—with an area reduced by 40 percent and a population by 30 percent?

No. Talking about economic problems makes no sense in the present day. Indeed, everyday life makes no sense in the present day. Indeed, everyday life is full of examples, statistics, and data that demonstrate that, even without having reached maturity, despite the sabotage imposed upon it in a hundred thousand ways by our ill-fated political

---

[47] A.N. Field: *"The Truth about the Slump,"* p. 65. Colbourne, Ibid., p. 45.

[48] Rector Leslie Gantt: *"The Gantt System,"* p. 59.

hacks, the machine is capable of supplying the West—and, if our tear-jerking globalists insist, all of Humanity—with all its vital and even secondary needs, a hundredfold.

"MANPOWER"

In point a) of the section titled "Statement of the Problem," we referred not only to raw materials but also to skilled labor, unskilled labor, and the scientific knowledge "sufficient to abundantly satisfy the needs of its inhabitants."

Human labor, encompassing that of researchers, executives, skilled, and unskilled workers, is given, in England and America, the generic name "Manpower"—the power or strength of man—which seems to us far more descriptive than the circumlocutions we use in Spanish to collectively refer to manual laborers, technicians, foremen, and executives.

According to official data, drawn from United Nations publications, while the population of Western countries increased by 14 percent, their "manpower" rose by 6 percent[49] during the period 1940–1970. Over the same time span, their food production rose, in absolute terms, by 21 percent[50].

In contrast, the production of industrial goods and services nearly tripled. It is impossible to know exact figures, and only approximations can be obtained, based on partial and comparative references. In any case, here too simple arithmetic supports the thesis that the workforce—whether skilled or unskilled—and production have increased more, in absolute and relative terms, than the total population of the West. From all this, the same conclusion can be drawn as when analyzing the impact of the Machine on the Western economy, namely, that the West should be experiencing a period of economic well-being—indeed, of true opulence—unparalleled in its entire history.

This, as far as the workforce is concerned, quantitatively speaking. For, in qualitative terms, our "manpower" has also undergone remarkable progress. The number, per capita, of technicians and skilled

---

[49] *Encyclopaedia Britannica*: Volume XXII. p. 795.

[50] Ibid. Ibid. Volume XXII. p. 797.

workers—in the worst-case scenarios (England, Italy)—is the same as it was thirty years ago[51] but it must be kept firmly in mind that in the 1940s, England was responsible for a vast Empire, a circumstance that, unfortunately for it and for Europe, no longer exists today. With regard to Germany, we have been unable to find comparative data, but progress is undeniable and well-documented in France and Spain, and even in the United States. In certain Western countries, such as Canada, the increase in the skilled workforce has been spectacular, on the order of one hundred percent[52].

[51] *Encyclopaedia Britannica*. Britannica Book of the Year 1969–70. p. 328.

[52] *Encyclopaedia Britannica*: Britannica Book of the Year 1969-70. p. 276.

THE DECLINE IN PURCHASING POWER

Despite, then, the marvelous progress of mechanization and the quantitative and qualitative advances in our "manpower," we find ourselves in the midst of a crisis, to use the established term. This crisis—and all those that preceded it—presents the surprising characteristic that the general abundance of everything necessary for human life coincides with general misery. Perhaps the term "misery" may seem excessive. It will not seem so to us if we stop to consider that a large portion of our fellow citizens—throughout Europe—live, as the saying goes, "hand to mouth," deeply in debt and always anxiously awaiting the end of the month with their bills due, while thousands of companies are on the brink of bankruptcy precisely because a huge number of those bills will not be collected, and millions of families living in this precarious situation are gradually swelling the ranks of the unemployed... There are surpluses of everything: agricultural products, manufactured goods, coal, steel, cement, iron ore, copper, tin—in a word: there is too much of everything. Why, then, do these riches find no buyers? Certainly not because of the buyers' ill will, of course, since these riches cannot be distributed for free. And therein lies the problem: consumers cannot reach the products; they cannot buy what has been produced. There is no money...

Why is there no money? This simple question has two answers, which complement one another. The immediate—though less decisive—answer is the one that immediately springs to mind: we could call it the Prostitution of the Machine to Labor. The truly decisive one—the hardest to see and the one that underpins the entire artificial scaffolding of the current economy—we will call the Prostitution of the Machine to Finance. We will address these later. We will begin with the apparent, yet absurd, Machine-Labor antinomy.

It is an undeniable fact that, in the West, thanks to our modern machinery and the forces of Nature that have been subjugated to man, wealth increases while the number of workers employed in producing it decreases. We thus observe, at the same time, an increase in production and an increase in unemployment. But since the unemployed, by simple definition, are those who are not paid, these unemployed are subtracted from the army of consumers, and the produced wealth piles up uselessly, and soon the need to curb its production—and even to destroy it—makes itself felt.

Classical economists kindly refer to this as a crisis. But it is no crisis. It is, quite simply, a revolution. The Industrial Revolution. A revolution that, among other things, has produced the following exemplary cases:

One man, with an excavator, replaces 25 men.

1 man, with a combine harvester that reaps, loads, bundles, and threshes, replaces 18 men.

1 man, with a Ketten loom for continuous weaving, replaces 20 men.

1 man, with a Raschel loom for continuous fabric, replaces 28 men.
1 man, with a cigarette-making machine, replaces 100 men.

One man, with a bottle-making machine, replaces 54 men.

One man, operating a massive computer that makes 60,000 entries in the General Ledger—recording the customer's number, the check amount, the balance, and the accrued interest—does the work of eighty bank employees.

One worker operating a shoe-making machine in Great Britain produced 67 dozen pairs of shoes per year in 1907. By 1930, with a more advanced machine, production had risen to 92 dozen pairs, and by 1970, to 140 dozen[53].

Based on cold, objective facts, we can demonstrate that the machine lightens, at a minimum, 95 percent of human labor. And it not only lightens it but, generally speaking, does it better. (We are speaking, of course, of industrial, mass-production work, without any artistic implications.) We would even assert that 95 percent is a conservative estimate. Let us leave it at that, however, as compensation for the human labor required to maintain the machines, even though such labor is often performed by other machines as well.

---

[53] M. Colbourne: "*The New Economy,*" expanded and revised edition by E. Leben Sheldon Emry: "*Billions for the Bankers. Debts for the People.*"

Let us ask ourselves honestly: What is the Machine's objective? And if we manage to shed taboos and prejudices, we will see that the answer, simple and concrete, is this:

> The purpose of the Machine is to supply the market with the greatest possible quantity and best possible quality of goods and services, while minimizing human manual labor.

Since the Machine is a labor-saver, its primary function consequently consists of throwing workers out onto the street. If, for the frayed nerves of this Vaseline-soaked era, the phrase seems excessively brutal, we can present it in a gentler form: it is the Machine's function to relieve the worker of the labor burden. It is evident that the worker thus "relieved" finds himself without work—or with barely any work to perform—and that his employer can do without him. And no less evident is that if the Industrial Revolution is not accompanied by a true Distributive or Remunerative Revolution, the blessing that the Machine ought to be turns into a curse. Although neither the machine nor James Watt can be blamed for this.

Let's take a simple example. Imagine a large family living in an enclosed space—for example, a secluded valley, or better yet, an island. The members of this family contribute to the common material stock according to their abilities. One fine day, one of them comes up with the idea of installing a turbine at the waterfall next to the house, thereby generating energy that allows everyone's work output to increase tenfold. The members of this family exchange the goods produced among themselves using vouchers that serve as a "measure" of exchange. With the arrival of the turbine, approximately nine-tenths of the members of our community are left without work, and the head of the family—a man, it seems, of a rather thick mind—tolerates that nine out of ten of his relatives—his subjects—are left without the essential vouchers—the currency of that community—and starve to death. Unless one fine day, moved by pity, he decides to burn the inventor of his turbine as a heretic and throw the turbine into the bottom of the ravine.

But let us suppose that, instead of being a staunch adherent of classical economics, that head of the household had heeded the advice of his eldest son, a man without prejudice, who explained the problem to him as follows: "If the turbine displaces nine out of ten of us from our jobs, that means our community gains, all at once, a power nine times greater than that of its natural resources. If we take this added power into account, to obtain the products we need we would have to pay nine times less than before the turbine was installed. That is to say, our cost of living should be nine times cheaper than it was when our work depended exclusively on our own muscles or those of our horses, mules, and oxen. Naturally, to reduce our cost of living ninefold, the people whose labor has been absorbed by the turbine and the energy it provides should receive, for their free time, as much as they used to receive for their work before the introduction of that blessed machine into our community. Being paid in this way—both as consumers and as producers—their purchasing power would increase, and the lack of manual labor among nine out of ten of our relatives would be more than compensated for by the greater output of the machines, powered by the turbine."

And if the head of the household, leader of that community, were to object: "How are we going to pay them, whether they are consumers or producers?... How can one pay for work that hasn't been done?...What will those who still work think—that is, those from whom the turbine hasn't taken away the possibility of working?"—his interlocutor would simply reply: "It's not a matter of paying those who work the same as those who don't; the former, obviously, would earn considerably more; but if those who aren't working now want to earn as much as those who are, they'll just have to figure out how to install another turbine on the Poniente waterfall. The possibilities for our community's development are still immense, and it doesn't all end with the turbine—it's only just begun. Besides, it's highly debatable that we should pay for work that hasn't been done. After all, who came up with the idea for the turbine? One of us, but that "one" didn't just spring up spontaneously in the midst of our community. He was cared for, educated, trained, given an education, and all of that, combined with his innate potential, allowed his genius as a r inventor to blossom. His genius, his qualities, belong to him, of course; the credit is his, but it is not his alone, and our community has no reason to be ashamed of the progress made thanks to the efforts of one of its members—besides the fact that it was not solely his effort and that, in isolation, without all the others, our inventor is of no use."

Let us leave the father and the eldest son to argue, as they always do, by the law of Life, about the Past and the Future. And let us return to the Machine, and to the so-called "overproduction," as if such a thing could exist in a Western world where so many people still lack the bare necessities. As if there were not people—and, what is even worse, so many high-and-mighty figures—who openly wished for poor harvests or deliberately limited industrial production. Are there not poor political novices, whom we shall assume to be well-intentioned, who set out to absorb unemployment? How can they be so blind as not to realize that unemployment is the measure of technical progress? We repeat: unemployment is the measure of technical progress. And all the efforts of producers tend to create more unemployment, because they all cut their overhead costs to the absolute minimum and, consequently, their production costs. Does anyone know an industrialist or a farmer who does not constantly rack his brains trying to ensure that the work done today by ten workers can be done tomorrow by eight?

And at a time when unemployment is breaking all records across the globe, in Spain, the so-called "Second Government of His Majesty" coldly announces that it will take measures to absorb it. But this government, whether it knows it or not, whether it wants to or not, is going to create even more unemployed. And if anyone doubts this, let them read its public works program: the countryside is to be electrified, which is, in itself, undoubtedly an excellent thing... but it will become disastrous if the necessary labor and financial measures are not taken simultaneously. Why? Because as soon as electricity appears anywhere, the motor is not long in following; as soon as the motor runs, thousands and millions of workers are left idle. So, with the best of intentions to eliminate unemployment, the only thing being done, under the present circumstances, is to increase it, either immediately or, at best, in the short term. And all this because of the stubborn refusal to turn toward the only solution to the problem of unemployment, which consists, on the one hand, in reducing the workday and, on the other, in adapting a financial policy to the situation posed by the growing power of the Machine—in a word, in making Money a medium of exchange, and not a commodity. If this is not done, the proposed electrification of the countryside— —will only exacerbate unemployment; that is, it will further reduce consumption, making the paradox of scarcity in the midst of abundance all the more glaringly apparent... Electrify the countryside, yes; but by putting Money at the service of the Machine—that is, by radically and completely revolutionizing our current economic structures. And does it seem logical that this could be achieved with a government that, rather than a government, resembles the Board of Directors of the Banco Español de Crédito, with the addition of other figures from the country's other major banks?

INFLATION AND DEFLATION

In this section, where we have attempted to explain the fundamental causes of the decline in purchasing power, we have referred to point b) of the Statement of the Problem, namely: that "poverty and scarcity exist because people do not have enough money to buy the goods produced by modern industry and agriculture at a price attractive to producers." And in point c) we stated that "when one lacks something of any kind, the most obvious remedy is to create it, and there is no physical difficulty in creating more money." This point was also touched upon in the preceding section, but we must return to it since it is the essential one, the "deus ex machina" of the current economic-financial system, based on the fact that Money, conceived as a measure of production and, therefore, a medium of exchange, has been transformed into a commodity and, as such, must obey the inexorable law that dictates that the price of a commodity is inversely proportional to its abundance. Thus, by creating more money, in a given situation, we reduce the value of the Money that existed prior to such creation. We emphasize the qualifier, "in a given situation," to which the staunch defenders of classical economics—conceived before Watt's invention, that is, in the era of Scarcity—cling like castaways to a lifebuoy. It is well known that when an amount x of new money is unexpectedly injected into a market, prices rise and money loses value in a proportion exactly equal to x. This phenomenon is called inflation, that is, the increase in the quantity of money without a simultaneous increase in the quantity of goods that this money is meant to measure and exchange. We alluded to this in point d), when we said that inflation "is, evidently, a calamity. But the gradual increase in money and goods so that the purchasing power of the former remains at the same level as production and prices remain stable has nothing to do with inflation, and is, after all, what we need."

Well, achieving that ideal gradual increase in money and goods has never been too difficult, and it is extremely simple today, thanks to the fantastic progress of information technology, which is capable of telling us with marvelous accuracy the quantity, quality, and value of the goods produced in a country within a unit of time. It is sufficien, then, to adapt the creation of new money to the new economic situation, so that it may usefully perform its function as an instrument of exchange. In other words, the National Statistical Services inform the Ministry of Finance that, in the first quarter of the year, goods worth x were produced, and in the second quarter, goods worth y are expected to be produced; then, money equivalent to the arithmetic mean between x and y is put into circulation[54]. We will discuss the mechanics of putting that money into circulation later. For now, let us limit ourselves to emphasizing that, as we outlined in point d) of our Statement of the Problem, since it is possible to know exactly the volume of production and its average rate of increase, the new money necessary and sufficient to prevent inflation can likewise be created. Before proceeding, we consider it useful to illustrate with a simple example what inflation and deflation actually are.

The first thing we must keep firmly in mind, both for the example that follows and for everything related to money under the present circumstances, is that the more of it there is, the less value it has, and the less there is, the more value it has. Let us suppose, then, that by some sort of biblical miracle—the miracle of financial manna—one fine day, upon waking, we realized that all members of a certain community had twice as much money as we had the day before. What would happen? Imagine that two farmers were planning to go to an auction to buy a tractor. Both genuinely want to buy it, and since each now has twice as much money as they did the day before, they bid higher than they had planned to before the "miracle." If we consider the entire community in which this "miracle" has occurred—and not just with tractors, but with houses, crops, and everything else—we will see that the result of all this, after a short period of time, has been that prices have doubled.

Now let's suppose the opposite scenario: that is, that one fine day, upon waking up, we find that we have exactly half the money we had when we went to bed. Our farmers will likely give up on buying the tractor, or, if anything, bid up to about half of what they had intended; gradually, the same will happen with other goods, whose price will stabilize at roughly half of what it was before the miraculous overnight manipulation.

---

[54] Obviously, the fact that it is done quarterly and using the arithmetic mean method. Past-Future is not mandatory, but a simple suggestion regarding what seems most expedient to us under current circumstances.

Fortunately, these changes in the value of money do not occur overnight, but they do happen quickly enough to create enormous problems. For example, when there is a lot of money—that is, during an inflationary period—anyone who has something to sell can raise prices without much difficulty. But those who depend on wages fixed for specific terms in contracts, or who have sold their crops before inflation sets in, or, quite simply, those who receive payment for an item sold on credit or depend on a government pension—these are the main victims of this situation. In the long run, of course, everything adjusts again: old contracts expire and are renewed on new terms, wages rise, and sometimes even retirees' pensions are adjusted. But while this readjustment is taking place, many go bankrupt and, in their downfall, drag others down with them—especially suppliers.

Of these two phenomena—inflation, or an excessive increase in the money supply, and deflation, or a decrease (or insufficient increase) in it—this is undoubtedly the worse, even though, in the long run, both are fatal. During a period of inflation, producers—or at least some of them—can at least keep their factories running and sell their goods with a reasonable expectation of getting paid. But in a situation like the one we are suffering from—that is, deflation—it is the producers who suffer the most; no one buys more than what is strictly necessary to "get by," due to a lack of money, and industries, and even agricultural and livestock operations, are failing by the thousands.

We have said that we are in the midst of deflation, and we suspect that such a statement will surprise most people, since in the wretched Western press of our time we are fed up with reading clichés such as: "the current inflationary situation," "the inflation rate is x percent," "unemployment caused (?) by the current inflation," etc., etc. We do not wish to wield St. George's lance to break down open doors. We will limit ourselves to suggesting that those who disagree open a dictionary and find out whether inflation is, or is not, "an excessive increase in the money supply relative to production," and deflation "an insufficient increase in the money supply relative to production." Then they can consult any Chamber of Commerce to see if there is low unemployment (an inflationary period), or high unemployment (a deflationary period), or if there are low inventories, or, on the contrary, if those inventories are at the peak of the curve. Finally, you can put it to the test: you can read the financial reports in the press and find out whether or not the banks have available liquidity, or "argent frais" (fresh money), as they say in the banking slang of our northern neighbors, or, simply, "money" as the man on the street says—meaning pieces of metal or paper issued by the government.

It will be argued that it matters little whether what happens to our impoverished economy is inflation or deflation, and that the essential point is that its health shows very alarming symptoms. Wrong. There is no cure without an accurate diagnosis. Problems must be solved based on a correct approach.

And if our ineffable economists, without needing to play the wise men, simply observing what is happening around them and using the common sense generously attributed to them, were to decide to correctly frame the problem of what they call the Crisis—instead of talking so much about inflation—they would say that the current crisis is the result of monetary deflation, the onset of which must necessarily coincide with the final period of credit inflation. Or, if one prefers less technical language, that (the crisis) is nothing more than the consequence of a shortage of real money in proportion to the amount of fake (or scriptural) money that has been created in previous years[55].

We will need to address this topic of Money in detail in due course, as it is the key to the current Crisis.

But we do not wish to proceed without drawing attention to the surprising fact—truly magical—of this permanent, constant, and universal "error" on the part of the self-proclaimed financial experts. Something incredible. Moreover, taken to that level and that "permanence," the error strikes us as impossible. The terms "error" and "permanent" are mutually exclusive; they cannot coexist; they are incompatible. Rather, it seems like obedience—conscious or unconscious—to certain directives from specific forces interested in diverting attention from the real problem. And if the reality were generally acknowledged—that is, that we are suffering from a deflation comparable only to that of 1929–1934 —also called inflation back then!—people might well ask why we are suffering from it and why the

[55] The fact that we are in the terminal phase of the so-called economic cycle means that all the symptoms of the new deflationary situation coincide with one of the previous, inflationary, one: the rise in the price index. The essential cause is the politically driven increase in wages at a time when production is slowing down. We will address this point in the section "The Prostitution of the Machine to Money."

State does not apply the simple and logical remedy, that is, inject a substantial amount of currency into the market to back the goods actually produced by the community and facilitate their exchange among its members. And that is precisely what they are trying to prevent: the appearance of fresh, or authentic, money, free from the inherent flaw of Debt. We have stated that we will address this—Credit and Debt-Money—in detail, as it is the crux of the problem. Now, we believe the time has come to digress and address other dead ends that, to distract our attention from the real problem, present themselves temptingly at our disposal.

THE FALSE REASONS

One of the reasons cited to justify the economic malaise of the West is the loss of the European states' colonies. A simple analysis of the facts shows us that this reason is, rather, a fallacy. Indeed, even if we take for granted and accept the circular argument that colonies were held for economic reasons—a crude and entirely false Marxist interpretation of Great Politics—it immediately becomes clear that the argument lacks any demonstrative value. The leading continental power in 1939, Germany, had no colonies, but England did, although they were in an advanced state of underdevelopment, with the exception of the white colonies of Australia, Canada, and New Zealand; and, in any case, those colonies did not spare it from the Great Crisis of 1929–1934, that gigantic deflation that began on Black Friday on the New York Stock Exchange, a deflation that, as we have seen, was renamed inflation for the sake of the Cause. In a word: Germany, without colonies, suffered the first Great Economic Crisis of the century, and also without colonies emerged from it, before the others, precisely because it had begun to implement a reform—or rather, a Financial Revolution—alongside the ongoing Industrial Revolution. England, with colonies, suffered that Crisis from which it emerged, only partially, during the World War—it is curious, but there is never that kind of crisis in the course of wars—and, with practically no colonies, is suffering it now, with the British Isles being precisely one of the focal points, geographically speaking, of the problem.

Something similar, though less pronounced, can be said of France and Italy. As for Spain, it cannot be said that its few and barren colonies pulled it out of any economic quagmire in the 20th century, but, in any case, Spain also suffered—with colonies—the consequences of the so-called Crisis of 1929 and is suffering them again—without colonies—in 1976. The economically powerful Scandinavian countries have never had colonies—unless one wishes to consider the ice of Greenland as such—and this has not spared them from the infamous Crisis either.

But the most definitive argument against that reasoning—which is not valid—comes from the United States of America itself. Indeed, the United States, which—whether labeled as colonial or not—exerts a political influence that is, by extension, economic, across numerous territories on all five continents, monopolizing markets as it sees fit, is also suffering the effects of the Crisis. In fact, the first major crisis of the century began in the United States itself, whose colonial empire already extended, at that time, across Alaska, Puerto Rico, the Philippines, Guam, Hawaii, the Aleutians, Samoa, and thousands of islands in the Pacific and the Caribbean[56]. And the second, the current one, began once again in the United States itself, following Nixon's initial move toward devaluation of the dollar until its actual implementation, beginning in the second half of 1974. And they remain in the midst of the crisis with all its consequences: economic stagnation, unemployment, and tens of thousands of bankruptcies. No. It has not been the loss—nor the acquisition, more or less disguised—of colonies that has caused the current Western economic crisis. And we repeat that we call it that as a concession to the mental inertia of the majority, since there is no such economic crisis, but rather a purely financial one. Another reason cited, with true insistence, to justify the Crisis is another "crisis"—the oil crisis. It is undeniable that the sudden and significant increases in the price of crude oil have dealt a serious blow to the economies of developed countries, which, from an energy standpoint, rely largely on oil.

However, it is worth bearing in mind that:

a) In 1929 there was no oil crisis, and yet an economic crisis occurred that was exactly the same as the current one.

b) The United States, the instigator of the current crisis, has sufficient oil—in its own fields and in those owned by Standard Oil of New Jersey, part of the Rockefeller trust, in Venezuela and Mexico—to meet its needs. Before the measures taken by oil-producing countries, Arab oil accounted for 10 percent of U.S. consumption, and it was purchased more for political than economic reasons. Uncle Sam now obtains that 10 percent from Iran, at more favorable prices. Despite all this, we repeat, the United States is not only suffering from the current crisis, but suffered from it before anyone else.

c) The Union of South Africa, Australia, and New Zealand have not purchased Arab oil for many years. They have been obtaining it for a long time now from Iran and Indonesia. Furthermore, they have their

[56] It is evident that, for practical purposes, it is irrelevant whether those territories were called, then or now, "states," "provinces," "colonies," or whatever. The name does not define the thing.

own oil fields—in the case of South Africa and, especially, Australia—so that the "oil argument" can hardly be applied to these countries. Nevertheless, all three have suffered—and continue to suffer—from the current economic crisis, which, for example, in the extremely wealthy Australia, has reached extremely high levels.

d) In any case, the radicalization of the so-called "oil policy" of the Arab countries occurred after the first symptoms of the Monetary Deflation-Credit Inflation we are experiencing. This began with the devaluation of the dollar in early 1973 and erupted with full force in September of that same year. The Arabs did not radicalize their oil policies until the spring of 1974. There can be no cause-and-effect relationship, therefore, as the latter must be chronologically later.

It is true that the policy of the Arab oil-producing countries has been a handicap for Europe; our continent has suffered more than anyone else from the consequences of the struggle between Zionism and Pan-Arabism, as this has dealt the classic "blind man's blow" that has only served to further enrich the colossal multinational companies, refiners, and distributors of crude oil, which are almost entirely under the control of individuals and interests linked to Zionism. On the other hand, it is highly doubtful that these Arab countries benefit at all from the rises in the price of their crude oil, since, being under-equipped and underdeveloped countries, they must import almost everything, and one need not be a financial wizard to realize that what they gain on one hand they lose on the other, in the form of spectacular price hikes on everything they must import[57]. Nevertheless, returning to what concerns us most directly—the West and its core, Europe—we must take the following facts into account:

1) Despite their threats, Arab countries have never ceased to supply oil to Europe, through distributors in 90 percent of cases, or directly in the remaining 10 percent. Only during the last Arab-Israeli war did the Netherlands suffer an oil boycott, which was more symbolic than effective (since the Netherlands could obtain Arab oil through any

[57] Although this falls outside the scope of the present study, we should mention that the only thing Arab presidents and petty kings have gained through their oil blackmail is the world's antipathy. And if one day they decided to push too hard, it would cost the powerful oil companies little to organize a Crusade for the benefit of Humanity... and the State of Israel—a crusade that would put an end to the arrogance of petty kings who have failed to understand that the primary political force in the 20th century is strength, not blackmail.

of its eight Common Market partners) and, in any case, by distancing itself politically from the United States and, in part, from the so-called "socialist countries," the Arabs have become almost exclusive customers of Western Europe, which has served as a safety valve for our national economies in their obsession with creating jobs.

2) In any case, this is not the first time that Europe, or a large part of it, has been deprived of oil. Indeed, if we use our memory—a faculty of the soul today as neglected as its companions, intelligence and will—we will recall that approximately thirty-five years ago, on a continent militarily dominated by Hitler, from the North Cape to the Pyrenees and from Brest to the Caucasus, there was not a drop of oil, with the exception of the Ploesti fields in Romania, which were regularly bombed by the British air force. Well, Germany and its allies obtained synthetic oil through the distillation of coal. It will be objected that the industry of that time had not, by any stretch of the imagination, reached its current level of development. To this one can respond by listing the enormous fuel requirements of an army as highly motorized as the Wehrmacht, and that needed to keep the Luftwaffe and the Kriegsmarine on a war footing, as well as that required for a war industry operating at full capacity under the bombs of the democratic-communists. And it would be an outrage to the European genius and its spirit of inventiveness to deny that what Germany accomplished practically on its own in the 1940s and during wartime, with its coal distilleries bombed daily, can—not merely be repeated—but surpassed in the 1970s, in peacetime... AND WITH GERMANY FLANKED BY ENGLAND, FRANCE, AND THE OTHER EUROPEAN STATES that are supposed to be free.

It is not that we deny, with the foregoing, that the so-called oil crisis has harmed the West, and especially Europe. But we do resolutely deny that it has been, not merely the cause, but not even a cause of the current economic crisis; at most, a temporarily aggravating circumstance. And we say "temporarily" because, aside from the aforementioned possibility of coal distillation, the mere occurrence of Arab blackmail was enough to immediately trigger oil exploration on our continent, with excellent prospects in the North Sea, the Aegean; off the coast of Norway, and even just a few kilometers from the Spanish Mediterranean beaches[58].

---

[58] This situation has, incidentally, served to highlight the lack of political stature among

LOCATION OF THE AFFECTED ORGAN

In the preceding sections, we have analyzed the five essential points of the problem, including a foray into the realm of economic fantasies—namely, the false reasons that are being imposed on us as the causes of the current Western "economic" crisis. From this analysis, we believe it follows quite clearly that we have more than enough production to meet our needs; that scarcity arises because there is not enough money to buy what is produced at a price attractive to producers; that it is obvious that if money is lacking, it must be created, and that this is by no means impossible; that inflation and deflation are impossible with the help of information technology, and that the machine, by fulfilling its function of relieving man of labor, leaves him with free time to employ his intellectual and spiritual energies, for if there is one thing we can be absolutely certain of, it is that there is a great deal of intellectual, spiritual, and recreational work to be done in a rapidly developing world, in which so much remains to be done in all fields. And one of the first things that must be done is, if not to beautify the machine, then at least to ensure that it is as attractive—or as unrepulsive—as possible; another is to combat the depredations inflicted on Nature, not by the machine itself, but by man's thoughtless use of it, concerned only with extracting maximum performance without calculating the harm caused to the ecological environment. In short, there are so many things left to be done that the word "leisure" can be ruled out of a future human society, organically conceived.

Having analyzed the five points of what, for us, constitutes the problem's framework, and taking for granted that our Economy is sick, the pertinent and logical step is to identify which organ or organs of the Economy are afflicted by this illness.

---

today's European leaders. A Pitt, a Bismarck, or a Richelieu would have understood, as Europe lost its foothold in the Middle East, that it was necessary to plan for future oil supplies and take the appropriate measures. Of course, this would have entailed expense and sacrifice... and democratic politicians cannot ask their constituents to make sacrifices, as this is not electorally profitable. Europe only began seeking oil once Arab blackmail began, and God only knows what political and economic concessions must have been made to Standard and Shell!

In reality, we won't have to look far. The Economy consists of only three components: Production, Consumption, and Distribution. Production consists of the goods and services that human labor and machinery make available to the people—that is, to consumers. Consumption consists of the needs, the desires for the less necessary, and even the superfluous, of the population. And Distribution is nothing more than the means that allows Production to reach Consumption in the most suitable way possible. Production is also called Supply, and Consumption, Demand.

Let us say, before proceeding, that the purpose of Production is Consumption. It is not to create jobs; it is not to balance the Balance of Payments; it is not to regulate prices. The purpose of Production is Consumption.

First, Production. We can consider it from three perspectives: that of machinery and facilities; that of the raw materials used to fuel it; and that of the "manpower" employed to supervise it, keep it in operation, and organize it. In the sections "The Machine" and "Manpower," it has been emphasized that the machinery of Production in Europe is in excellent health. Indeed, there is apparently a surplus of machinery and facilities, since many of them are idle. We do not believe this to be the case, but in any event, it poses no problem for Europeans to expand their manufacturing, agricultural, or livestock facilities whenever and however they wish. As for "manpower," the trend shows a steady increase, despite social and political unrest (university strikes, etc.). Finally, regarding raw materials, aside from the new oil discoveries on our continent, we have coal for centuries; we are pioneers in the development of atomic energy—even though, so far, the main beneficiaries have been Russia and the United States—and also of solar energy and tidal energy, and in the Netherlands there is natural gas for all of Western Europe.

Second, Consumption. We have already said that Consumption is Demand, that is, what keeps the wheel constantly turning. There is nothing wrong with Consumption, or the desire to consume, or, as professional economists call it, effective demand. No matter how much armchair revolutionaries rail against the so-called "consumer society," parroting the slogans of those who benefit from the current situation, there is nothing reprehensible about a community seeking to consume what it has produced through its own efforts. This organ, then, is healthy.

Finally, Distribution, which is the organ that articulates, that establishes the connection between Production and Consumption. It is evident that if the problem lies neither in Production nor in Consumption as such, the organ of the economic body that is affected by the problem is, by process of elimination, Distribution. Money is the means through which Distribution operates. This is a classic definition. But perhaps it is not as absolutely precise and exact as the subject we are dealing with requires. For us, Money is the means through which Distribution ought to operate. In reality, as things stand in our ailing economy, the operating mechanism of Distribution is Finance. Finance is the means that allows—or does not allow, as it suits the financiers—Production and Consumption to meet.

THE DEVIL'S BRIDGE

It is essential to have a completely clear understanding of this linking function performed by Finance. An example that illustrates this function in an unsurpassably vivid way is provided by the so-called "bridge example," which has been used by at least five writers[59]. A bridge that, due to the strange and harmful things that occur on it, we will call the Devil's Bridge.

This bridge connects the two banks of a river, which represent Production and Consumption. The bridge, of course, is Finance, and the traffic that passes over it consists of goods and services—that is, the wealth of a community. And we take it for granted that in every economic system, apart from children, the elderly, and the disabled, everyone leads a double life; that is, they are both producers and consumers. Thus, an industrialist produces, for example, steel ingots and consumes food, clothing, etc., and a farmer produces grain and consumes seeds, tractors, as well as the services of retailers in the central market and, of course, also a portion of his own grain. That is to say, everyone works on the bank of Production and lives on that of Consumption.

The bridge has the following characteristics:

a) It is a structure designed to allow traffic to cross the bank, and nothing more.

b) It was built for the exclusive benefit of the community.

c) Apart from the service it provides, it lacks any artistic value; it is nothing more than stone, steel, cables, and scaffolding.

d) It is a human creation, not a divine one, and consequently any modifications that its better use may make advisable can be introduced into it, and, as Colbourne says, "it should not be revered either for the benefit it brings or for the fact that it was an extraordinary thing for our

59 "*The Green Magicians,*" by Thomas Porter.—"*The ABC of Money,*" by Felix J. Frazer.—"*The New Economy,*" by Maurice Coulborne.—"*Le Crédit Social et le Catholicisme,*" by G. H. Lebesque.—"*The Paradox of Capitalism,*" by Richard R. Morrisson.

grandparents"[60].

e) It belongs to the community that needs and uses it, and not to the private that maintains it to collect tolls.

f) Consequently, it is the responsibility of the owners of said bridge to make all decisions they deem necessary for its normal operation and to hire the staff responsible for carrying out those decisions; this staff will, of course, be paid by the bridge owners and will be accountable to them for their performance.

And yet...

Let's look at the very strange things that happen on this diabolical bridge. To do so, let's compare them, paragraph by paragraph, with the things that should happen on a well-managed bridge.

a) It is a science whose purpose is the acquisition of political power. At present, there is not a single government in the world that is not composed, essentially or in the majority, of front men for High Finance. The governments of the so-called socialist countries are not excluded from this assertion, as we shall see later.

b) The bridge is viewed as if, instead of having been built for the benefit of the community, it had been built for the benefit of those in charge of collecting the toll, for Money has become just another commodity, subject to the vicissitudes of business, rather than an instrument of measurement and exchange.

c) To contribute to the collective deception, the bridge has been shrouded in a golden legend, according to which, to cross it, users must be guided by the advice of magicians, experts in the arcane mysteries of banking.

d) Even though the bridge is a human creation, it is treated as if it were a pure emanation of divine will—so far removed, then, from our capacity for understanding, that instead of widening the bridge to accommodate traffic, it is precisely the traffic that, to the detriment of the entire community, must conform to the bridge's immutable dimensions.

e) The bridge does NOT belong to the community that needs and uses it; rather, the instruments of Finance—that is, the banks—are private entities, including so-called national or central banks, such as the Banque de France, the Bank of England, the Federal Reserve

[60] M. Coulborne: Ibid. Id. Op. cit.

Bureau, etc.

f) Consequently, the bridge's employees are not appointed by the owners(?)—users, nor are they paid by them, nor, logically, do they report on their management to them. Quite the contrary, they reap immense personal benefits and, at the same time, political power, for their own benefit.

Later on, we will see that many more strange things still happen on that Devil's Bridge. But one thing is clear: the bridge does not function as it should. Well, when poor management causes traffic to grind to a halt and turn into a veritable chaos, the logical thing to do is to hold those responsible for its maintenance accountable and, if necessary, fire them. But that is not how it happens in reality; quite the contrary, people are led to believe that the only way for things to go well in the future is to keep the bridge's employees in their positions of privilege. Any debate about the economic function of Distribution—that is, of Finance—is taboo for our economic experts. So have decreed the financial Buddhas who pay them their meager wages.

MONEY

It is curious to observe how individuals highly versed in various branches of human knowledge display such profound ignorance when it comes to the subject of Money. In general, whether learned or ignorant, the only thing they know about Money is that they are always short of it. In an era like the present, when those who control so-called public opinion draw people's attention to topics as unusual as they are exotic—Atlantis, extraterrestrials, prehistory, parapsychology, "paranormal" phenomena, ancient "Eastern wisdom," and a very long list of others—it seems strange that, just as in archaeology, history, and philosophy, they are—and we do not criticize this a priori—true revolutionaries; yet, when it comes to addressing the topic of money, which is of such vital interest, our "opinion makers" are genuine reactionaries. For them, the old concepts of Medieval Economics still hold sway—they, of all people, so progressive!

For them, Money is a commodity, but it is evident that Money, as a medium of exchange—which is what it is and nothing else—must be, above all, stable, and a commodity will only be stable as long as its supply is well balanced with its demand, and this cannot, logically, be of interest to a money dealer, since what interests him is for demand to far exceed supply, so he can raise the price of his commodity.

What is money? Money is nothing more than a means used as a calculator or counter of wealth. As a medium of exchange, its value derives from its acceptability. Charles A. Lindbergh, Sr., defined it as "something that has reached such a point of acceptability that it does not matter what metal it is made of or why people desire it, for no one will refuse to take it in exchange for goods or services"[61]. It has also been said that money is like a universal ticket. A theater company, a railroad, or a city bus company issues its own tickets, the possession of which entitles one to use the services of such companies. Well, money is, we repeat, a universal ticket or, put another way, a claim by its holder against his fellow citizens ; a claim whose origin is, precisely, work that

[61] Charles A. Lindbergh, Sr.: "*Banking and Currency and the Money Trust,*" p. 81.

has been done for the community.

But the best definition is given by Sir Arthur Kit Son when he says: "Money is the Nothing that is obtained for Something before it can be obtained for anything"[62]. Let us examine this: Money is Nothing, that is, a piece of paper whose intrinsic value is zero. It is obtained for Something, that is, for work done for the community, and with it one can obtain anything that belongs to that community.

We have said that Money is a medium of exchange: more precisely, it is the medium of exchange. All producers devote their time and energy to providing goods and services useful to the community. The things they produce, without consuming them themselves, become available to the community. In exchange, they receive money, which is like a claim on goods that others have produced. As the instrument of exchange, money likewise becomes the instrument of measurement. Money measures a community's wealth, exactly in the same way that the meter measures lengths and the kilogram measures weights. Based on that indisputable principle, the value of a currency must remain stable. If this is not the case and if prices skyrocket, always winning the race against wages, it is due to the manipulations of the sinister officials at Devil's Bridge. The time has come for us to examine the "modus operandi" of these gentlemen.

---

[62] Arthur Kitson: *"A Fraudulent Standard,"* p. 69

THE BIG SCAM

The vast majority of people imagine that a bank is a respectable and safe place to deposit money, or to go and borrow money that other people have deposited. However, banks lend up to nine times more money than they actually keep in their vaults. How is this possible? Because banks, in reality, do not lend anything. They merely make it appear so. When a bank lends money—or, to use banking terminology, extends credit—all it really does is accept the borrower's credit. We will explain, striving for brevity and clarity, how this genuine scam is perpetrated, for it is indeed a scam since all the elements of such a crime are present in its execution.

Although the banking business and its corollary, usury, date back to the time of Babylon, banking in its modern form emerged in Europe in the early 17th century, first in Lombardy and the Netherlands, then immediately in England, followed closely by the other countries of our continent, and finally in the United States shortly after its establishment as an independent nation.

In those days, those who possessed gold and silver—metals that, due to their relative scarcity, were best suited to serve as legal tender in times of scarcity—would entrust them to a banker for safekeeping, who would store them in a safe. Obviously, it was neither convenient nor safe to go about constantly carrying gold and silver—or the coins later made from both metals—and, moreover, it was advisable to keep the money in a bank, equipped with a sturdy safe, constantly guarded by an armed guard. The banker thus provided a service, and for that service it was logical that he should charge—we say "charge"—a fee. Upon depositing their money at the bank, depositors received a receipt from the banker, and it was on this receipt—a document, in itself, beyond reproach—that the greatest scam of all time would be orchestrated.

In fact, the banker was an observant man and soon realized that people were using those receipts as if they were real money. Those receipts, backed by real money, served the same function as money—that is, they were used to purchase goods and hire services. Since these receipts were not registered to a specific person, anyone—who might never have deposited money in the bank—could go to the bank's teller window and, by presenting a receipt for a certain amount of official or legal money, demand that amount on the spot. An essential point: we say official or legal money because these receipts, upon being accepted by the community as a means of payment, automatically became, in effect, money. The banker also realized that, on average, depositors withdrew only ten percent of the money deposited over a given period of time. In other words, ninety percent of their deposits remained in his vaults, and the remaining ten percent was sufficient to cover the receipts that would be presented for payment. The temptation was too great for the banker, a man whose conscience was not overly burdened by scruples—or perhaps he could not feel them due to his ethnic and religious background. And he asked himself the following question: Why not put more checks into circulation, representing nine times the value of the money he actually had in his safe? For him, asking that question in this way was equivalent to answering it in the way his inner self desired. That is to say, he multiplied his promissory notes by nine—committing himself to pay money he did not have, or, at most, had only one-ninth of—and began lending it to individuals and, above all, to merchants, charging interest on that nonexistent money. In reality, rather than nonexistent, it was fictitious; for it did have an existence, albeit a fraudulent one, as goods and services were delivered on his behalf. This was the original fraud, which has endured to this day, and which lies at the root of all our economic ills. As Gertrude Coogan says, "bankers may justify their practices however they please, but the fact is that when they lend their 'credit' at interest, all they do is create private money, which they can then reclaim and destroy at will, to the borrower's despair and impoverishment"[63] who is periodically forced, due to the artificial scarcity of credit-money, to hand over real goods in exchange for the credit-money he borrowed.

By proceeding in this manner, the banker has, in effect, created money. And to create it, all that was needed was for a bank employee to take a pen or a ballpoint and write in the bank's General Ledger ( ) any figure—let's say ten million pesetas—in the borrower's debit balance. But at the same time, the collateral that the borrower had to offer against the bank loan was recorded in the borrower's credit balance. This collateral, which must always be a tangible asset—a house, land, crops, or the title to a business—is always worth more than the money the bank lends. The borrower is given a checkbook, which

[63] Gertrude M. Coogan: "*Money Creators,*" p. 18.

allows them to conveniently divide the loan amount into smaller amounts; then, interest on the loan is charged to their account—interest that ranges from five to nine percent during relatively "calm" times, but which can be much higher during turbulent times—and the transaction is set in motion.

Let us pause for a moment to make the following observations:

a) By effectively putting more money into circulation—money that appears on the market before it has had a chance to generate more wealth—an inflationary process has been set in motion; that is, the money already in circulation has lost value.

b) The goods that will appear on the market with the new money will have their cost burdened by bank interest—as we have already said, ranging from 5 to 9 percent—which consumers will ultimately have to pay. This is a further contribution to the inflationary process.

c) While the banker has handed over his "promises to pay" money—for no one, however much of a banker he may be, can create something out of nothing, and thus what he lends are nothing more than promises—the borrower, on the other hand, has handed over to the banker securities representing wealth that, apart from being far greater than the loan, is real. There has thus been a flagrant breach of trust on the part of the bank. As we noted elsewhere[64] "while the bank holds against the community collateral representing real wealth, such as factories, estates, crops, etc., the community holds no collateral against the banks. The slightest attempt by a bank's creditors to enforce their guarantees against it reveals that such guarantees, in fact, have no substance whatsoever. If such creditors "put too much pressure" on the bank, they are punished by losing all their savings. The bank closes its doors, revealing that its "promises to pay" are false promises... unless the government comes to its aid with a moratorium.... a moratorium whose consequences will be that, in the end, the community as a whole will have to pay to cover the banker's false promises." The objection that this very rarely happens is completely invalid. If it happens rarely, it is because in every country there is a Higher Banking Council[65] whose primary mission consists, precisely, of correcting excessive deviations

[64] J. Bochaca: "*Finance and Power*," Omnia Veritas Ltd.

[65] Naturally, the names of such organizations vary: in the United States, this organization is called the Federal Reserve Bureau; in other countries, there are so-called Clearing Houses, etc.

from the permanent credit inflation by ensuring that no bank exceeds the fateful ratio of 9 in the division between outstanding loans and the money recorded in checking accounts. And when, nevertheless, a bank goes off the rails and crosses the danger zone threshold, the others come to its aid, since the financial system functions as a whole—on a national scale for ordinary matters, and on an international scale for major economic problems. But that aid, ultimately, will be paid for by the people—that is, every citizen who goes to the market—for, as we have said, and this must be kept firmly in mind, so-called bank charges are included in production costs.

As demonstrated in sections a) and b), by creating an inflationary situation, the bank has robbed each and every member of the community. The fact that banking activities have been legalized by the government in every country does not in the least diminish their fundamental illegitimacy. The fact that a State, or a hundred States, decree—as the frontmen they are for High Finance—that the private creation of Money is legal when carried out by a bank and illegal when carried out by a counterfeiter does not in any way alter the fact of its radical immorality, from an ethical standpoint, and its ineffectiveness, from an economic standpoint, except, of course, the private economy of the banks and their minions.

And as demonstrated in section c), not content with stealing from the community, the bank has committed, against the client to whom it has granted a loan, a true breach of trust, by exchanging a promise worth, say, X minus the interest charged in advance, for a reality (titles to tangible assets) worth at least X multiplied by two. And let no one object that the customer is perfectly free to accept or reject the "exchange" proposed by the bank. The customer is convinced that what the bank " ly" lends him are the savings of another fellow citizen and that for this loan one must pay a fee, called "interest." But the bank's activities do not end here; in reality, the disastrous effects of its activities are scarcely significant when compared to what follows.

Let's go back to the moment when the bank—or rather, the banking system, since all banks act in concert—has extended loans amounting to as much as nine times the money they actually have on hand. For now, the system seems to be working. The general euphoria masks the theft that has been committed. For it is evident that a genuine theft has taken place; by creating new money, the banker, just like a common counterfeiter, has stolen a little from each of his fellow citizens and has earned interest on the stolen "money"[66]. Thanks to the sudden issuance of new money, new wealth has been created, commerce is in full swing, and the "full employment" dreamed of by all has been achieved. Every time a borrower repays a loan to the bank, with its accumulated interest, the bank hastens to put it back into circulation. What classical economists call a "boom"—known in Latin countries as "market euphoria"—has taken hold. Prices are skyrocketing, while all kinds of products are offered for sale[67]. But the banker realizes that this price rise continues only as long as loans keep being made. Every time the banker stops making such loans—or, in other words, stops creating new money—prices stop rising, and as they stop rising, business collapses. The possibility of continuing to do more business in a bull market has vanished. Why? Because now the banker begins to find himself in trouble, since the volume of his loans is already hovering around 900 percent of his cash reserves. He now runs the risk that any demand for real money from his depositors, which for whatever reason might arise at any given moment, will expose to the entire community the true scam to which it has been subjected by the banker in question. Every loan he has issued, represented by checks, as well as every receipt he has issued to his depositors for the money they have temporarily entrusted to him for safekeeping, represents a promise to pay in gold and silver (currently the government's legal tender). That is to say, both his depositors and his borrowers can demand, at any moment, genuine money—that is, official currency issued by the state—in exchange for their receipts.

What is left for the banker to do in this situation? Only one thing: to cancel a substantial portion of the loans he has extended. Consequently, he summons to his office some of the industrialists to whom he has lent his "promises to pay" and invites them to repay, say, half of the loan. The industrialists will likely protest; they will not understand the banker's sudden demand at a time when everything seems to be going swimmingly. However, in the end, in the face of the banker's increasingly firm insistence, they will have to repay the requested amount. To convert their inventories into cash—the money the banker is demanding with such sudden haste—the industrialists will have to sell at any cost; that is, they will have to sell off a substantial portion of

---

[66] J. Bochaca: *"Finance and Power,"* p. 11

[67] Ibid. Id. Op. cit., pp. 12–13.

them at a loss, and at the same time, they will be forced to demand immediate payment from some of their customers who had purchased their goods on credit. The entire operation will trigger, in a cascade effect, a series of losses for industrialists and commercial intermediaries and, as a consequence, will lead to a general reduction in the volume of business—that is, ultimately, unemployment.

But this is only one aspect of the matter, since, in many of the situations that arise, manufacturers are unable to liquidate their inventories when and how the banker demands, and the bank enforces the collateral it holds against them, thereby seizing, in exchange for nothing—since it lent them nothing but false promises—real assets, which thus, with all the legality and all the immorality in the world, become the property of the bank.

Normalcy has returned. Meanwhile, many industrialists and merchants—more of the former than the latter—have gone bankrupt. Prices for all goods have risen; wages, inevitably, have too, but less so. A large segment of society, especially the so-called middle classes, has become a little more proletarianized. The only winner across the board is the banker. He, who has done nothing except perpetrate large-scale currency counterfeiting, has reaped immense profits in tangible assets and, more importantly, has seen his power to continue creating money at the community's expense confirmed, making him the most powerful man in the country. Moreover, in the height of cynicism, he even allows himself to severely admonish his fellow citizens, telling them that the recent crisis occurred because they wanted to live beyond their means. The simple objection that the community merely intended to consume what it had produced through its labor is utterly disregarded. The general ignorance regarding financial matters, carefully cultivated by the frontmen in its service, is the wall of silence against which common sense and popular instinct crash, as they vigorously reject the idea that a large portion of a community's members have been ruined precisely because they have worked too hard and, through their labor, produced a supply of goods that has not yet met the demand for them.

Normalcy has returned, we said. Our banker can now set the Great Scam machine in motion once again. The sheep of the human flock are already ready to be fleeced once more.

BANK CREDIT

In the genesis of the Great Scam, we have mentioned the word "credit" on several occasions, usually in conjunction with another word: "financial." Let's analyze this.

The word "credit" derives from the Latin "credere," which means "to believe." In short: the credit of something or someone is nothing more than the trust it inspires—if it is a person—or the belief in its ability to do what is expected of it—if it is a thing. The credit of a community is, therefore, the rational belief in its ability to produce, distribute, and consume the goods and services its members require. It is clear that the ability to do these things depends exclusively on realities such as the talent of the community's members and their capacity for work, as well as the resources of the land and subsoil of that community. It does not depend, in the least, on the number of banknotes that community decides to print, nor on the amount of gold that country hoards in the vaults of the central bank.

It should be crystal clear to any independent mind that, in any community other than a psychiatric asylum or the present capitalist-communist world, money must be based on the figure representing that community's real credit. Then, and only then, would the term "financial credit" no longer be a misnomer. On the contrary, it would be the only name that should be given to money, since financial credit would then be the reflection, in banknotes, of real credit[68]. In a word, the figures would reflect the facts exactly. In reality, however, in our sad reality of "Misery in Abundance," financial credit has nothing to do with real credit; rather, it is nothing more than a multiple of the gold held by the banks. Thus, our money, instead of being based on goods produced by honest labor, is based on gold. Even more tragic: sometimes it is not even based on that, but on pure fiction, on the assumption that people will not realize that the banks are counterfeiting money, building, on top of the authentic banknotes issued by the State, an inverted pyramid

---

[68] Maurice Colbourne: "*The New Economy,*" p. 379.

of "credits" nine times larger than it is supposed to be.

Furthermore, since it is issued by the banking system on the condition that it be repaid with interest, financial credit becomes a commodity, tradable like any other. The nation's currency becomes a commodity, subject to the same market forces that govern other goods, including the law of supply and demand. The basic function of money—that is, to serve as a medium of exchange and a measure of the goods and services produced by the community—is thus completely distorted.

And now, let us return to the banks, the creators of money.

The basic function of banks consists, in practice, of transferring funds from one of their checking accounts to another. This, naturally, is done by subtracting from one account and adding to another, through a simple arithmetic operation. The fact that the accounts may be held at different banks is of no consequence, because, as is well known, banks work in such close cooperation through clearinghouses that they function almost as if they were a single bank. It is essential to bear in mind that banks transfer entries representing money, not actual money—that is, paper currency issued by the state.

A check is an order given to the bank to transfer money—in reality, as we have already said, entries representing money—from one account to another. Money, in the form of metal or paper, is very rarely used in banks. In Spain, 85 percent of transactions are made through the check system. In the United States, 95 percent. Cash is used to pay small bills, to go to the market, for entertainment, etc. But major payments—rent, taxes, installments, etc.—are increasingly made by check.

Banks hold credit money in circulation when they make a "loan," but in reality, they do not lend anything. When the bank makes a "loan," the borrower agrees that, if they do not pay by the due date, their property—called collateral, which is worth much more than the credit they are requesting—will become the bank's property. The bank, therefore, commits fraud by recording the borrower's asset on the credit side of its books, even though it is not yet theirs and may never be. The borrower must then borrow that same credit (wealth) from the bank, paying ex interest. The credit is then transferred from the bank's account to the borrower's. In fact, according to a principle of fairness, the borrower's asset should be recorded in their own account to begin with. The bank then guarantees the borrower's payments up to the amount of the loan, which is always less than the value of the asset serving as collateral. The borrower begins to pay their bills with the "money" in their account, using checks. At the risk of repeating ourselves, we remind you that banks only transfer entries of wealth, or, if you will, of money, but not money in the form of metal or paper currency. "The loan began as an entry made with a pen or pencil in the bank's books, representing the borrower's property as collateral. Although technically nothing prevents it in exceptional cases, a bank never hands over coins, banknotes, or anything of value when it makes a loan"[69].

Banks use the banknotes and coins deposited by their depositors as reserve funds, which are never lent out. What they lend is an amount that fluctuates around 900 percent of such reserve funds. The interest paid on this credit-money is unduly charged and constitutes an immoral profit. Why is it immoral? Because, if credit—as we defined it at the beginning of this section—a nation's real credit consists of both the nation's potential wealth and the ingenuity and industriousness of its inhabitants, when the banker extends a "credit" to someone and charges interest on that "credit," he is doing nothing more than "lending" them something that is already theirs, with the added insult of charging them interest on it. It is as if someone were made to pay rent for the use of the house they inherited from their father... Banking practice could be justified if bankers lent not a multiple, but a sub-multiple of their total reserves—for example, half or two-thirds—retaining the rest to meet the normal demands of their depositors, and charging for that loan, which could then be called such, since it would be made in paper money, a rent—that is, non-accruing interest—of 2 or 3 percent at most, and the guarantee, or collateral, would be of a value similar to the amount of the loan. The system in question would be far from ideal—since the ideal consists, fundamentally, in money being an instrument of measurement and exchange, but not a commodity—but at least it would avoid the economic chaos we are currently suffering, the cause of which is none other than the private creation of counterfeit money. But what cannot be justified in any way is the current banking practice, which constitutes the most fabulous business ever conducted and ever to be conducted, consisting of the following:

---

[69] Thomas Porter: "*The Green Magicians,*" p. 5.

a) With one hundred monetary units belonging to a third party, "loans" are "opened" for nine hundred units. Borrowers are, for the time being, required to surrender, as collateral, securities representing approximately one thousand five hundred units.

b) Those nine hundred units accrue 9 percent interest (sometimes, with premiums, discounts, and other pretexts, more than 10 percent), meaning that their net return after one year is 81 units.

c) The depositor, whose money the banker has blithely gambled away, is given 0.5 (although in deflationary times, which they call inflationary, it may reach 0.75 or even 1). In other words, those 100 units, which have cost the bank 0.5 units per year, have earned it 81 in the same period of time.

d) From this, it follows—if the math doesn't lie—that the return on this stunning Ali Baba-style business is 16,200 percent. And this is with other people's money.

Does the so-called man on the street know that a good textile business, for example in the synthetic fibers industry, yields, in so-called times of prosperity, 7 or 8 percent on the capital invested, which naturally belongs to the business owners? Do you know that, in the metallurgy sector—and we are speaking, as in the previous example, of Spain—profitability rarely reaches 5 percent? Have you been informed that in England, in the cotton sector, profits did not reach 4 percent even in good times, while today losses exceed that percentage and companies are going bankrupt by the hundreds? Have you not read, in the daily press, long lists of companies that must suspend payments, precisely because their creditors do not pay them either, while on such lists the name of a single bank never, EVER, appears? And hasn't it struck you that while producers are going bankrupt and consumers cannot consume what everyone's labor has produced, banks are springing up like mushrooms on the facades of the finest buildings in the cities, and their balance sheets always show enormous profits?

Don't you think, dear reader, that it is shameful that a community which, through the labor of its members, has produced wealth waiting to be consumed, is told—as Mr. Villar Mir did in Spain and Mr. Chirac in France—that it has been living beyond its means and must tighten its belt? Is there anyone capable of providing a plausible explanation for this notion of "living beyond our means"? Because, naturally, those in question, who must have seen it very clearly, neglected to explain it to us mere mortals. The sharp-eyed journalists must have seen it crystal clear as well, and in Spain we witnessed the comical spectacle of the general bashing to which this Villar Mir was subjected, for half a dozen "political" reasons, absolutely harmless, while not a single hack asked him for a single explanation regarding this business of "living beyond our means" and "tightening our belts."

And, to conclude, for now, on the subject of bank credit, a simple demonstration—yet another—of its complete unviability.

Let's suppose that the money, which we'll call A, in a given community, is sound money, free from the burden of Debt. (For in our strange modern world, most money, created by banks, is born in the form of Debt, which must be paid off precisely when it is most needed—that is, at the very moment it should be used to distribute what has been produced.) Well, one fine day, the banks begin to create credit money, the interest on which we will call B. That debt, that is, "B," will be charged into the cost of all goods. It is clear that the community's real money, "A," cannot buy what has been produced, which will cost "A plus B." Well, actually, there is a way. It consists of the bank creating more credit money, which we will call "C." Everything would be perfect, were it not for the fact that "C" is born with a Siamese twin: its interest, which we will call "D." So neither A plus C can buy something that costs A plus B plus C plus D. They will muddle through as best they can, until the moment arrives when Abstract Money—as it is also called—exceeds "A" by a factor of nine. Then the cycle comes to an end: the bank calls in a large portion of its loans, seizes vast amounts of real wealth, and the next inflationary cycle can begin.

ON A GLOBAL SCALE...

Now that we have outlined the activities of the "domestic" banker—that is, the man who invents money that does not exist but from which he extracts interest that his fellow citizens are forced to pay—it would be useful to examine the other aspect of banking activities.

The "international" banker extends credit to firms engaged in trade with foreign countries: import or export companies, freight forwarders, shipping companies, customs brokers, insurance companies, etc. It is in this banker's interest for the volume of foreign trade to remain at a healthy level, in order to ensure the continued acceptance of his loans. It is evident that when this gentleman's colleagues, the "national" bankers, find themselves at the beginning or middle of the inflationary cycle—that is, when they are granting abundant credit and the fateful ratio of 9 is still far off—the volume of exports tends to decrease, since people can purchase goods produced within the country itself, and the country exports only its surpluses. In that case, the "international" banker has an interest in the "national" bankers reducing their loans. In reality, he does the same as the "national" banker, that is, he grants credit to companies involved in foreign trade, and even to foreign countries, so that they may purchase from his own country, for amounts that multiply, approximately, by nine the total of his current account holders' deposits[70].

It was inevitable that the "national" and "international" bankers would eventually agree to cooperate, since their operations, aside from being governed by the same mechanism, complement each other admirably. Consequently, when the domestic market is in full prosperity—that is, in the midst of credit inflation—the "national" banker receives full support, or "credit," from his colleague, the "international" banker. And when prosperity is followed by the cyclical crisis— that is, monetary deflation, the "national" banker, as he calls in his loans, extends a portion of them to his "international" colleague, who finances exports and who, moreover, in such circumstances,

---

[70] J. Bochaca: "*Finance and Power,*" Omnia Veritas Ltd.

receives aid from the alarmed government, which sees exports as an means of providing work for the masses who are growing restless. This is when tax breaks, export subsidies, and other forms of direct and indirect support appear. It could be argued that the government has no reason to react in this way and, instead of aiding the national or international banking scam, it can curb its activities, preventing the creation of uncontrolled money on a national and international scale, and creating it itself, in accordance with the volume of goods awaiting consumption. The argument is very appealing and entirely valid in another world or under different circumstances. In this world, and under these circumstances, MONEY MEANS POWER, and since Money—and, what is far more important, the power to create it—belongs to Finance, it follows that the Administration[71] is at the service of Finance, and not the other way around, as it should be. And any public official, no matter how high their rank, knows full well—or rather, intuits it, feels it in their very skin—that any hint of independence on their part in the face of the all-powerful forces of Finance will set in motion a mechanism that will begin with a media campaign against them and end with a letter from their superior "thanking them for their service." That superior must act this way, either because he himself is tied to the System, or because he knows that, if he supports his subordinate, he will, without a doubt, lose the next election.

To set this intimidation mechanism in motion, there is no need for secret meetings of hooded figures, nor Sanhedrin covens with black wax candles and cabalistic incantations, decreeing the civil death of the disobedient. The System works so well that, except in exceptional cases, not a single word needs to be spoken. Anyone who disrupts, or might disrupt, the functioning of the Financial Fraud machine is automatically punished, likely without those carrying out the punishment even realizing it.

[71] That word is gradually replacing "Government," and it seems fair to us since, at present, in our residual Europe, as far as government is concerned—what is meant by GOVERNMENT—we cannot bring ourselves to see any.

THE GOLD STANDARD

Everyone has heard of the Gold Standard. But no one has been able to give a clear explanation of what it is. Or, more precisely, of the reason for its existence.

Before the Machine appeared, precious metals—silver and, more commonly, gold—served as a medium of exchange. They preceded the advent of paper money, and in that era, which we might call one of Scarcity, or at least relative Scarcity, they served the purpose assigned to them.

Today, national currencies are based on gold. It is evident that, in a healthy economy, they should be based on commodities, but this does not suit the interests of finance, because the gold standard ensures the price that can be demanded by the omnipotent[72]. It is clear that as long as someone controls the supply of gold and money can be created only on the basis of it, that person will control the monopoly of money.

The best current definition of the gold standard has been provided, in our opinion, by Colbourne and the Scotsman Douglas: "Gold is an international measure of exchange." We admit that it is a brief definition and, above all, an incomplete one, but nothing more accurate can be said. If anything, one might add that in times of Scarcity, when goods were difficult to obtain and appeared slowly on the market, it could fulfill its mission—albeit very imperfectly—but, in the end, it could serve its purpose. But in the current Age of Abundance, the Gold Standard, objectively speaking, can be defined as nothing more than an incongruity. Today, the currencies of all countries should have no standard other than Labor. If the Gold Standard remains in force, it is to favor the interests of its holders and because the old fetishistic superstition, so deeply rooted in the human heart, regarding its divinity, has not wavered despite the catastrophes it has caused.

We have said that gold is an international measure of exchange, and

[72] M. Colbourne: "*The New Economy,*" p. 156

we will illustrate this with a simple, everyday example of international trade. Let us begin by noting that, since official money—that is, a nation's paper currency—is based on the gold it possesses, when a significant amount of gold leaves a country, paper currency is immediately withdrawn from circulation in an amount equal to the value of the gold in question. In other words, an amount of purchasing power disappears from the domestic market, equal to the gold leaving the country. Such a loss of purchasing power will cause prices to fall and put the brakes on the "boom" or prosperity before it becomes a danger to bankers. This is standard practice in all countries, which is why a decline in gold reserves—which occurs when imports exceed exports—is considered a disaster, as it means the balance of payments is in deficit. This withdrawal of paper money to compensate for the gold leaving the country can be carried out by proportionally reducing the value of the paper money periodically printed by the state through the Mint, or simply by raising taxes.

Since bankers are money traders, they place their loans where they can obtain the highest possible interest rates, provided, of course, that this is compatible with the security of repayment. And here, a side note: even in international trade, bankers demand their famous collateral guarantees.

Well then: let's suppose a Swiss banker lends one billion Swiss francs to the Colombian government so that it can purchase a couple of thermal power plants. And let's also suppose that the Italians produce them more cheaply than Swiss manufacturers. What will happen, then? Well, the Colombians will buy the thermal power plants from Italy; Italian technicians will travel to the Colombian highlands with the necessary equipment, proceed to assemble the plants, and the Swiss banker will pay the Italians. But the payment must be made in lire, since Swiss francs, in principle, are of no use to the Italians. In short: the banker will have to buy lire with Swiss francs, and then the lire will rise in value, becoming more expensive, while the Swiss francs will fall in value, becoming cheaper, on the foreign exchange market. And why is that? Well, because, as is well known, the more the demand for a commodity rises—and money, for a financier, is a commodity—the more its price rises. So if the lira rises too much relative to the Swiss franc, it will be more advantageous for the financier to use his Swiss francs to buy gold and then use that gold to buy lira. And, under such circumstances, gold will leave Switzerland. Then, one billion Swiss francs, in banknotes, will disappear from circulation. And prices will fall. And wages, too[73]. The consequence of this decline will be that the Swiss will then be able to produce cheaper thermal power plants, like the Italians do, or even better ones. Then Colombians, or whoever else, will be able to buy those goods in Switzerland, and the gold will not have to leave the country.

The consequences of this financial policy, as logical as it is disastrous, are as follows:

a) International finance can pit peoples against one another.

b) It can drive down the wages of the working classes in all industrialized countries.

c) Consequently, it can prevent any people from having sufficient purchasing power to buy their own goods and force them to export them in competition with all other countries.

d) This means a struggle for control of foreign markets, and, indirectly, perhaps war. Gottfried Feder[74] and, with an important qualification, Francis Parker Yockey[75] reach this latter conclusion. Indeed, according to Yockey, war occurs only for political reasons; only Marxists believe in wars for economic reasons, but if a non-political motive can create an existential tension between two peoples, establishing in them the friend-enemy dichotomy, then the motive becomes political and war breaks out, with that motive receding into the background.

---

[73] The idea that wages are falling will—we suppose—make many people smile. In reality, falling wages are a common phenomenon today, although they do not appear in that form, but rather in the form of the elimination of overtime or, simply, unemployment.

[74] Gottfried Feder: "*The Struggle Against High Finance*."

[75] Francis Parker Yockey: "*Imperium*," Omnia Veritas Ltd. www.omnia-veritas.com.

CENTRAL BANKS

The concept of the Gold Standard is inseparable from the existence of so-called "central" banks, institutions that, despite their name and official trappings, are in reality private, run by private individuals who are their true owners.

Although the first "central" bank to appear in Europe, in the 17th century, was the Bank of England, its predecessor must be sought in the Bank of Amsterdam. Founded by a Jew expelled from Spain, Fernandez Carbajal, this bank was the first to give its clients a "receipt" or "voucher," which could be detached using a system that was the precursor to today's checkbook. These "receipts," naturally, were given in exchange for money that was deposited for safekeeping in a safe. These are the famous receipts we have referred to repeatedly—receipts lent out up to nine times their face value. Like all precursors, it ended badly. The Bank of Amsterdam was a martyr to the sacred banking cause. Because, one fine day, it declared bankruptcy. The danger for banks lies in their very nature, and, at the same time, in human nature. The nature of banks lies in obtaining the maximum possible return on the money they lend, and human nature—all too human, Nietzsche would say, in the case of bankers—encourages money professionals to take ever greater risks, recklessly approaching a nine-to-one ratio in the deposit-to-loan ratio, and sometimes bankruptcies occur, though in such cases, it is generally the state that steps in with a moratorium to save the situation and prevent the ruin of depositors, and, as a consequence, also saves the banker. Of course, the banker's fate would not be that of his unfortunate clients, since basic prudence would have led him to keep his own money in a safe place or invest it in sound securities. Even the banker's fellow citizens who are not his clients have had to collectively pay, on a pro rata basis, for the actual embezzlement committed. This, of course, creates unpleasant situations. As a safety valve to prevent—or at least make as difficult as possible—bankruptcies, "central" banks were conceived.

The Bank of England was founded in 1694, through a charter granted by William II to a Jew from Amsterdam, Manasseh- ben-Israel. This charter was based on an earlier one, granted by Oliver Cromwell to Ali-ben-Israel, also from Amsterdam. Cromwell, who had received financial support from the Jews of Amsterdam in his struggle against the Crown, repaid the favors received by authorizing them to settle in England and pay 4.5 percent interest to anyone who deposited gold in their vaults (an exorbitantly high interest rate), which they in turn would lend to the government at 8 percent[76].

The reason for the creation of the Bank of England was a loan of one million two hundred thousand pounds sterling to William III. The Bank's methods were not new; they merely followed precedents. And the precedent was the usury practiced at that time by the goldsmiths of London[77], who were already operating clandestinely before the legally authorized Ali-ben-Israel. Those goldsmiths, who used to lend at ten percent interest, initially viewed the new Bank with suspicion, as it "only" lent at 8 percent—though this would soon rise to 9 percent—while the interest paid to its depositors would be reduced to half a percent.

The Bank of England, whose official name was "The Governor and Company of the Bank of England," introduced an innovation with respect to the practices established by the Bank of Amsterdam. It began issuing notes for the amount the Government owed the Bank; a privilege granted to the Bank by a Government grateful for the services rendered on several occasions by the Bank[78]. Thus, in gratitude for those services[79], the Bank was granted the authority to issue money. But real money, and not just promises to pay money, as the "pioneers" of Amsterdam had done, or, later in England, Ali ben Israel with Cromwell's consent.

The Bank of England—we repeat, a private entity—literally manufactured money. If the Bank had ten pounds of gold in its vaults

---

[76] Francis Parker Yockey: "*Imperium,*" Omnia Veritas Ltd.

[77] These moneylenders were a group of Lombard Jews who settled in England after being expelled from Milan due to their usurious practices. The street where they settled, "Lombard Street," is still occupied by their successors.

[78] Maurice Colbourne: "*The New Economy,*" p. 136.

[79] Such services consisted of massive support from International High Finance for the British Empire until the end of the 19th century. In England's struggle against the Netherlands, Spain, the France of the late Capetians and that of Napoleon, and the nascent Prussian Empire, Finance was an ally—certainly not a disinterested one—of England.

and lent five to the Government, it could produce a five-pound note and put it into circulation, thereby increasing the ten pounds to a total of fifteen; the government, which used five, and the Bank, which had ten—five new and five old—and the total amount could be in active circulation[80], a significant mass of money, without any new wealth having yet been created to justify it; in other words, inflation was occurring.

But the main function—the essential one, we might say—of the Bank of England and the other central banks that would emerge in every country was not to create money, but, above all, to perpetuate, with the support of the law, the modern banking system; that is, to ensure the continuity of illegitimate banking activities.

The "modus operandi" is as follows: The "central" bank lends to private banks[81] legal tender or government bonds or any other fully secure asset. In deliberately confusing banking terminology, the word "deposit" means "loan," and this is expressed in the well-known Anglo-Saxon banking phrase "A loan creates a deposit" when ordinary people would be inclined to believe that a deposit is money placed in a bank for safekeeping[82].

Well, deposits at the Central Bank, or loans from the Central Bank to private banks, are cold, hard cash—they are legal tender—because even when they are government bonds, they can be immediately exchanged for legal tender. The Central Bank, as the issuer of legal tender by virtue of an unprecedented privilege granted by the government, will always pay with legal tender to those entitled to it. Private banks, therefore, lend their customers promises to pay money up to nine times the amount of deposits that they, the private banks, hold at the Central Bank, just as they lend promises to pay money up to nine times the amount they hold on hand. For banks, cash, "," and

---

[80] M. Colbourne: "*The New Economy,*" p. 138.

[81] In reality, central banks are just as private as any other; we use this phrasing to highlight the difference between them.

[82] The mental poverty of the economic critics we have to put up with can be so incredible, and their ignorance of banking matters so crass, that one sometimes comes across statements like this in the financial section of a newspaper: "A reading of Bank So-and-so's balance sheet reveals the public's confidence in its management, as the volume of its deposits has tripled in just three weeks" And the sky isn't falling!

deposits at the Central Bank are, in reality, the same thing... However, there is a difference between them. Cash is cash. It is legal tender. But, as has been said, deposits at the Central Bank are loans from the Central Bank. Said Central Bank, like all banks, issues promises to pay legal tender. But it can, also like all banks, call in its loans or reduce them substantially. It can do so in various ways, and the effect of this is to reduce all the "deposits at the Central Bank" of all private banks and, consequently, the amount of legal tender of each and every private bank. When a private bank loses legal tender, it must also cancel or reduce its loans so that it is never at risk of lending promises to pay money in an amount exceeding nine times its holdings of legal tender[83].

An example: A private bank holds, at a given time:

In Checking Accounts...................................100 million

In Deposits at the Central Bank.........................100 million

Total..200 million

That bank will issue promises to pay up to 1.8 billion.

But the Central Bank cancels 50 percent of its loan, and then the private bank has:

In checking accounts....................................100 million

In deposits at the Central Bank..........................50 million

Total..150 million

That bank will now lend 1.35 billion in promissory notes. A side note. You may have noticed that we refer to bank loans as "promissory notes" to pay money, because that is what they actually are. We have already seen that banks only lend promissory notes, which are also false, since the slightest attempt by borrowers to turn them into reality—that is, by demanding real money for them in an amount exceeding ten percent of the total value of such promises—reveals that

[83] R. McNair Wilson: "*Promise to Pay*," Omnia Veritas Ltd, www.omnia-veritas.com

the bank has committed a breach of trust, that its promises are false, and that, consequently, it must post a "Closed" sign on its teller window. But let us continue with the mechanism of how Central Banks operate.

That mechanism, through which private banks borrow from the Central Bank, allows the latter to control them by increasing or decreasing the amounts of legal tender. This control is exercised for the benefit of the entire system, since central banks, by virtue of their position, their volume, their semi-official status, their connections with the central banks of all countries—connections that transcend real or fictitious national political rivalries—and their ability to manage gold; in short, by virtue of their very importance, are uniquely positioned to see, above the clamour of the money market, when their colleagues at private banks are taking excessive risks and may be approaching a critical situation.

Central banks are, therefore, the coordinators of private banks' activities. They also serve as a safety valve and a guarantee of their profitability, and, ultimately, as the custodians of the gold standard, which is the cornerstone of the entire system on a global scale.

In 1844, the Banking Act was signed in London and approved by the British Parliament, mandating that England's gold reserves be deposited with the central bank—that is, the Bank of England. This had already been the practice for nearly two centuries, but the financial sector demanded the backing of the law, and shortly thereafter, the traditional alliance between the British Empire and international finance began to crack. Traditional Anglo-Saxon legalism guaranteed the financial sector its positions in England, and it now felt free to act with greater flexibility in its global policy. Thanks to the Banking Act, money was officially free to "find its own level," that is, it could be invested abroad if it was advantageous to do so, provided that higher returns could be obtained there within a reasonable margin of safety. Another consequence of the Act was that the export of gold, when it occurred, was bound to cause a shortage of money in the domestic market. We have already discussed this in the section on the Gold Standard. This in y shortage of money in the domestic market inevitably leads to a drop in prices, thereby forcing employers to reduce wages in order to remain competitive.

The convertibility of paper into gold—which is what the Gold Standard is—at prices governed by the law of supply and demand, is a system that must, necessarily, engender misery. Domestic industrialists and farmers find themselves trapped in a vicious cycle. The only thing they can do to remain competitive is to cut their workers' wages or increasingly automate their operations—which, sooner or later, means laying off a certain number of their employees. But precisely because they have lowered wages or reduced their workforce, it will be very difficult—perhaps impossible—for them to sell all their products in a market whose purchasing power has fallen, precisely because of those lower wages or that unemployment. Domestic producers must, as far as possible, orient their production toward exports. And so, a system whose original purpose was, in theory, to serve domestic needs is driven, by the force of this disastrous system, toward the production of goods cheap enough to compete successfully in foreign markets. This is the purpose of International Finance: Foreign Trade. No country is allowed to live for itself. On the contrary, each country must compete against all the others, so that the profits reaped by Money are as great as possible everywhere.

What does the "gold standard game" consist of? It is based on the exchange of goods between two countries. Countries, like individuals, are both producers and consumers. Thus, Spain can sell oranges and manganese to Germany, and Germany, at the same time, sell machinery and chemicals to Spain. The oranges and manganese will be offset by the machinery and chemicals. It is clear, however, that this ideal balance of trade cannot always be achieved with absolute precision. For example, it is quite possible that Spanish oranges and manganese are worth more than the machinery and chemicals received in Spain, in which case, at the end of the year, Germany would find itself with an unfavorable trade balance with respect to Spain. How can the Germans balance it? Obviously, by sending more machinery or chemicals to Spain, but it is possible that the Spaniards are no longer interested in those German products, or find them cheaper elsewhere, for example in Sweden. The gold standard offers a solution to the problem. The Germans can send gold to Spain to settle the debt, because gold is accepted on the spot, worldwide, as a means of payment. Every currency is convertible into gold at a certain exchange rate, and the holder of gold can buy any currency at a specific exchange rate[84]. This payment in gold would be no more significant than a simple settling of accounts were it not for the fact that all the world's currencies are based

[84] R. Mc. Nair Wilson: "*God and the Goldsmiths*".

on gold. If this were not the case—if all currencies were not based on gold—Spain, in the example cited, would have more gold, and Germany less, but this would have no effect on either Spanish or German domestic prices. However, the effect that will actually occur as a result of the settlement of the account through a payment in gold, on both German and Spanish prices, is based on the rule that when gold leaves a country, an amount of money from that country equal to the value of the gold that has left must be withdrawn from domestic circulation. That is to say, an export—an outflow—of gold causes the Central Bank to "withdraw" banknotes from domestic circulation equal to the value of that outflow, thereby forcing it to reduce its loans (the "deposits at the Central Bank") to private banks, which, in turn, must cancel or reduce loans made to local industry, and deflation will occur in the domestic market. In other words, when a country must use the gold standard to balance its trade balance—technically called the Balance of Payments—there is a contraction in the money supply in that country, equal to the amount of gold lost.

We know that demand, or the purchasing power of a country's domestic market, depends on the loans extended by banks to the industrialists, farmers, and ranchers of the country in question. But loans are—or rather, function as—money, and the amount of money in a country, as has already been stated, depends on the amount of gold held by that country's Central Bank. Thus, purchasing power must depend on the amount of gold held in the vaults of the Central Bank. If, according to the laws of this convoluted system, gold must leave a country to pay for an excess of imports over exports, the money supply in that country will decrease, following this cycle:

a) The volume of bank credit will decrease.
b) Consequently, the volume of production will decrease.
c) Logically, industrial profits, workers' wages, and shareholders' dividends will decrease.
d) Also logically, purchasing power will decline, and consequently,
e) Product prices will fall. And then a vicious cycle ensues. The drop in product prices causes a drop in wages and, in turn, in purchasing power.

In other words, a system has been devised whereby when gold must leave a country, the prices of consumer goods must also be reduced and wages lowered. A very important point: Prices do not need to fall in absolute terms, but rather in relation to the cost-of-living index. It is quite possible that governments, frightened by popular discontent, will decree political wage increases, which are nothing more than stopgap measures—as is happening, especially, in Spain—although the final result is, inevitably, a drop in prices. In any case, this price reduction makes that country's products more attractive—more marketable, or more saleable—due to their low cost; as a logical consequence, people in other countries buy them in greater quantities, and thus the volume of exports increases[85]. The country in question now finds itself with a balanced, or even favorable, balance of payments and is therefore in a position to receive gold.

That is to say, in principle, the "mechanism" of the gold standard balances itself out, or, if you will, corrects itself. Suppose gold enters a country: in that case, the money supply increases, bank credit to production increases; production increases; demand increases, and prices rise. Consequently, wages must also rise, until a point is reached where products become too expensive to compete in foreign markets[86].

In this way—so claim the advocates of the gold standard—uniformity and price stability are achieved throughout the world. But this is not the case, as the facts demonstrate. BECAUSE GOLD OWNERS LEGALLY RETAIN THE FREEDOM TO WITHDRAW IT FROM CIRCULATION, CREATING A GLOBAL SHORTAGE. There may also be the case of a sudden discovery of new gold deposits anywhere. The gold standard system has no provision for such contingencies. Ultimately, it can be demonstrated experimentally that the gold standard is of no use in keeping prices—and wages—stable. Later on, we discuss the case of Germany between 1933 and 1939, at the time World War II broke out. GERMANY DID NOT HAVE A SINGLE GRAM OF GOLD, AND ITS PRICE INDEX FLUCTUATED OVER SIX YEARS, BY 0.4 PERCENT, WHILE ENGLAND, WHICH POSSESSED ENORMOUS AMOUNTS OF GOLD, SAW ITS DOMESTIC PRICES RISE BY ELEVEN PERCENT OVER THE SAME PERIOD. Moreover, as we will see later, not even that modest 0.4 percent should have occurred; if it did, it was due more to political causes—Hitler had to take into account the

[85] Gertrude M. Coogan: "*Money Creators*".

[86] Gertrude M. Coogan: "*Money Creators*".

international situation and the pressures he was under—than to economic ones. From this experience, as well as from the case of Japan—another country that disregarded the gold standard—it follows that gold is completely unnecessary for stabilizing prices, but it is necessary for the owners of gold, for if the world were to stop using it, they would suffer grave harm if people realized—which would inevitably happen—that gold is not only unnecessary as the basis of currency but is completely unsuitable for that purpose, especially in an age like ours, when the production of all kinds of goods exceeds gold production by several thousand times. The owners of gold would then find themselves deprived of their instrument of domination. Only as long as the public believes that a bank is lending it real, tangible gold will it agree to pay nine percent on its loans. But the moment it realizes that this is not true, it will understand that the bankers are swindling it through the simple system of creating counterfeit money.

It is sometimes argued that, after all, the borrower gets what they want—that is, the means to purchase goods or services or pay off debts—and that is what matters. But this is not the case, for, aside from the fact that only those who have actually earned money should, in principle, have the right to lend it, one must take into account the fact that any creation of new money diminishes the value of existing money. Thus, when the state creates new money to pay for public works, civil servants' salaries, military armaments, and other expenses arising from its specific function, the value of the money in existence prior to that creation is evidently diminished to some extent; however, this inflation is offset by a reduction in state taxes, since these are levied solely to pay for state works and services. In contrast, the interest paid to banks is a true private tax, which yields no benefit whatsoever to the community.

In short, the Gold Standard is justified today solely as a regulator—through "central" banks—of the creation of Debt-Money by private banks and the enslavement of all countries to the irresponsible power of International Finance. How is the latter achieved? Through the system, made official by law in virtually every country in the civilized world, whereby all gold reserves are held in "central" banks, and these banks and governments issue legal tender only in proportion to the gold they hold. No government can create gold; consequently, no government can issue money, nor even invent it as any banker does when granting a loan. In this way, the owners of money, as McNair

Wilson states[87], are in a position to "force all borrowers in the world—that is, all producers, employers, or wage earners—to produce as cheaply as possible in order to pay the highest interest rates on loans, without forgetting, of course, to secure the necessary collateral. As can be seen, they are in a position to intimidate those governments that show a tendency to become unprofitable debtors, whether by failing to balance their budgets or for other reasons, including political ones." In such cases, the owners of the gold—an international "clique" whom we will identify later by name—demand it from the relevant "central" bank in the form of bullion, thereby forcing the latter to repay its loans to ordinary, so-called private banks, which, in turn, through the mechanism of the System, must do the same with their victims (their customers). Prices fall, and ruin and bankruptcies ravage the country. Or else the governments intervene, dictating or authorizing political price hikes, and prices rise, but wages remain stagnant or rise less, and the consequence is even worse: ruin and bankruptcies continue to ravage the country until the entire accursed cycle is completed, and moreover, retirees and civil servants are left destitute, the concept of saving is discredited, and vast segments of the population are proletarianized, especially the long-suffering and vilified middle class.

[87] R. Mc. Nair Wilson: "*God and the Goldsmiths*".

THE SUBVERSION OF THE NATURAL ECONOMIC ORDER

Napoleon has been described by many superficial historians as a mere conqueror, little more than a "condottiero" concerned only with securing positions of renown and fortune for himself and his large family. As Yockey notes,[88] his philosophy of the State has been ignored. But his economic ideas were clearly expounded by him to his loyal followers Caulaincourt and Las Cases, who, in their "Memorial of Saint Helena," reproduce the following phrase from the Great Corsican: "Economics is Production, not Trade; it is based primarily on Agriculture; secondarily on Industry; and finally on Foreign Trade."

We sincerely believe it is impossible to improve upon this definition of the economy, which is brilliant in its simplicity. It is evident that the first and essential task in the digestive system of an organized community—that is, in a national economy—is to ensure that the body of that organic entity exists, that is, that it is nourished. At the risk of stating the obvious, we dare to affirm—or rather, to remind, since it has been forgotten—that no one will eat a crankshaft, a tractor, or a bar of iron… or even gold. The first, the essential, is agriculture. And not only from a primary, existential point of view, but also a spiritual one. Agriculture signifies the bond between people and their homeland; it is the very life of towns and villages, it is the roots to which we belong. Hatred of cities as such is irrational, but we believe that cities without a ring of cultivated fields are like trees without roots.

There is no doubt that none of the above is intended to disparage Industry. If Agriculture is essential for existence—that is, for survival—Industry is essential for living, materially speaking, and for carrying out a "Great Policy," as Spengler put it, if we are to refer to the total, that is, political, aspect of the Nation.

Finally, in the natural economic order, as articulated by Napoleon, comes foreign trade. The purpose of foreign trade is to import from

---

[88] Francis Parker Yockey: "*Imperium*," Omnia Veritas Ltd.

other countries what cannot be produced —or is too expensive to produce—at home, and to export abroad the country's own surpluses that may be needed there. As Napoleon said: "Agriculture is the soul, the foundation of the Empire; Industry provides the comfort and material happiness of the People; Foreign Trade is the superabundance, and allows for the free exchange of the surplus of Agriculture and Industry[89]. In very exceptional cases, in countries that are very poor due to their climatic conditions, such as Switzerland, exports may predominate, whether in the form of services (tourism) or precision instruments. But such cases merely confirm the general rule, as exceptions that they are, and in any case, we must remember that, as we explained in the section "Scope," we are concerned with the economy of the entity called Western Civilization, which is—or should be—economically self-sufficient.

The Napoleonic view of exports is that exporters—save for exceptional cases—manage on their own. This is logical. Export is overabundance; it is luxury. There is nothing wrong with luxury, provided it is honestly earned, of course. But it is irrational to sacrifice oneself for luxury. And that is precisely what is done on a daily basis, and on a global scale, within the absurd Gold Standard System and International Capitalism.

Why?

Because, contrary to the natural, organic system of the economy, Capitalism and High Finance, through their transfers of credit to foreign countries that can provide greater profits, manage to strip domestic markets of their purchasing power, thus forcing producers to export goods they have no chance of selling—due to an artificial scarcity of purchasing power—in their own country. Thus, foreign trade comes first, and if it languishes—in the given situation, under current economic and financial conditions—the country goes bankrupt. Industry and agriculture are unconditionally subordinated to the demands of the export market. Ultimately, workers and peasants likewise become dependent on the export market, since a rise in wages would affect production costs, and this would have an adverse impact on the ability to place domestic products in foreign markets. For this reason, the natural economic policy pursued by Germany beginning in

---

[89] Las Cases: "*Memorial of Saint Helena,*" p. 185.

1933 provoked such a tremendous reaction from international high finance. By gradually curtailing the ability of private bankers to grant credit—that is, to create money—the German government succeeded in stabilizing prices. At the same time, and as an indispensable complementary measure for its foreign trade, it liberalized currency exchange rates, allowing its exporters to fend for themselves, though—admittedly—with the backing of a currency, the Mark, which was based not on gold but on the labor of a hardworking, intelligent, and tenacious people. And this is the opposite of international financial practice, which demands:

a) A floating price scale, achieved through credit-driven inflation and deflation—the source of so-called economic cycles—thanks to which the financial sector reaps fabulous profits and, at the same time, absolute power.

b) Fixed exchange rates, which are only changed when it suits the merchants of Money.

On the other hand, Finance is infinitely more interested in Industry than in Agriculture.

Why? Simply because greater profits can be obtained from the former. Industry depends on machines. Agriculture depends on unpredictable factors, such as droughts, hailstorms, pests, and epidemics. Even though the industrialization of agriculture can improve its yields, everything has a limit. That limit is harder to reach in industry.

The result of applying the mechanics of the financial system to the economy thus transforms all economic values. Profit takes precedence over what is useful and even what is necessary. Foreign markets receive the primary attention of governments. Next, they focus on industry, which can mass-produce goods for export. Last comes the poor relation: agriculture.

What a despicable parody of what should be genuine, healthy, normal trade! Other countries are exploited and enslaved with vast sums of financial credit that can no longer be lent within the country itself, to be used elsewhere so as to yield profits for the lords of Gold, while the country's stocks run low and everyone is eager to consume what they have produced! Financial export through foreign credit is not honest trade with other countries, but rather forcing them to take on obligations; it is a scam, a deception designed to profit from the creation of money on an international scale and, ultimately, a cunning means of gaining control over another country that has been driven into debt. Bank debt, which is, by definition, unpayable unless one takes on—to cancel it—a new debt, larger than the previous one. And the apostles of the System present this as a contribution to understanding among peoples! But what do we see everywhere? On a global scale, governments of noble nations squabbling like suburban greengrocers over market share, creating pre-war tensions. And on a national scale? Well, on a national scale, the same thing happens in every country. Industrialists are clamoring to lower wages, directly or indirectly, in order to be competitive in foreign markets. Strikes break out. Employers, when they can, respond with lockouts. Naturally, workers get angry with their employers. Employers, with their workers. But both are at the mercy of unknown financiers, who control the amount of money in the market. Under these circumstances, a large portion of the working class will be left without work, unless wages are reduced—which is materially impossible. And if they are not reduced—directly or indirectly—many companies will go bankrupt, and in any case the workers will be left without work. And when, at last, a large part of society—workers and employers, farmers and day laborers—has been ruined, then the horrendous cycle of Prosperity-Crisis-Prosperity-Crisis can begin all over again. In such tragic circumstances, can anyone be surprised by the hatred between the "classes"? Or by workers against employers? Or by employers against workers? Or by nations against one another?

No one sees the true enemy. No one sees the Great Parasite. Or they do not want to see it. No one seems to want to realize that the root of all economic evils lies in the false promises to pay put into circulation at interest by the Parasites. No one seems to want to admit that if money, on a global scale, were real, and not fake, there would be no need to fix exchange rates or to make the tremendous efforts that are made to prevent a demand for Gold exceeding ten percent of what has been lent. Thus the natural economic order is subverted. And peoples are pitted against peoples, nations against nations, races against races, so that the most monstrous system of theft that the human mind (?) has managed to conceive may survive—to establish the tyranny of th r that coven of witches that is International Finance.

DEBT

To describe our current financial system without mentioning Debt would be as difficult and absurd as summarizing the tragedy of Romeo and Juliet while omitting the rivalry between their respective families.

The best definition of our financial system has been provided, in our view, by the Scottish Commander Douglas, according to whom it is "a system aimed at creating unpayable debts"[90] and we would take the liberty of completing it by adding: "... and precisely because they are unpayable, all the states of the world remain permanently subject to the clutches of said system."

When we speak of debt, we are not, of course, referring to the debt that an individual, or a private or public entity, may incur with respect to another person or other entities, but rather to the system as a whole, according to which all money in existence is a debt owed to the banking system. Anyone in the Western world who has, say, a million units of currency in their checking account may believe they actually have it, if that makes them happy. But in fact, they have no more than a few thousand, at most, because even though that million appears as a credit in their bank account, in another bank's account it will appear as a debit, as a debt, because that money was created as a debt.

And if at any given moment all the depositors in a country were to go to their respective banks and demand, in hand, either the totality of their deposits in cold, hard cash—that is, in legal tender—or a receipt, legally authenticated by a notary, specifying that the money they deposited in their checking accounts is invested in this or that company or has been lent to the government itself—they would be in for the unpleasant surprise that the most they would receive (in cash or authentic receipts) is ten percent of their money. And this is in the best-case scenario, for if the banks had even slightly "run wild" in their issuance of fiat money, they would receive only about five percent. That is to say, in our crazy system, human labor, goods, and services are paid

[90] Ch. Douglas: "*The Control and Distribution of Production*".

for in what the French call (monkey money), that is, in something purely non-existent. In other words, they are not paid for, or are paid for at only five or ten percent of their real or agreed-upon value. What people understand as "money"—that is, banknotes and metal coins—is nothing more than "small change."

Money, which should be a MEASURE, is DEBT. And unpayable debt.

Why unpayable? Because of interest.

How can the world pay back more money than has been created as a loan? How is it going to pay back 109 when there are only 100? And those 100, moreover, exist only "in the abstract." The world is not a miracle worker.

How, then, is this problem solved? How can a system survive when its very results inevitably create such a problem?

The answer is simple. The problem is not solved; it is postponed, put off, and kept alive through the application of a whole complex of subterfuges, palliatives, and expedients, namely:

a) Through corporate bankruptcies and insolvencies.

b) By resorting to suspensions of payments and sales below cost price, in order to obtain cash.

c) By throwing themselves into the mad rush of exports, in which it is impossible for everyone to win, but it is very likely that all exporters will lose when, to stay in the race, they must resort to "dumping"[91], which also ruins the domestic market of importers.

d) Through the practice of sabotage, that is, the curbing of production. And, as the culmination of the entire structure...

e) Through the creation of new debt-money, that is, more unpayable debts.

Bankruptcies and "dumping" breed misery and worker unemployment. Exporting at any price gives rise to national rivalries that can lead to wars. Sabotage of production halts progress. And with

[91] "Dumping": selling at prices below the cost of production.

the constant creation of Debt-Money comes tyranny over individuals, peoples, and nations: over the entire world. The modern states themselves, which are usually so meticulous in everything concerning the "external signs" of their sovereignty, find themselves totally subject to this disastrous system and, consequently, to its beneficiaries—that is, to International Finance. The principle of fiat money issued abusively to banks, to which we allude in the section "Central Banks," means that states, however powerful they may be—or believe themselves to be—are irrevocably subject to the financiers: to "Money Power," as they call it in America. Later on, we will see, in very specific and current cases, to what extent of abject submission modern states can be driven by the financial system we are suffering under. The debt of states—and we are obviously not referring to that which they may have incurred with another state, but rather to that derived from the creation of Debt-Money—is so staggering, so unbelievable, that even by squeezing their unfortunate subjects with brutal and absurd taxes, they cannot even manage to pay the annual interest accrued on such debt.

THE PROSTITUTION OF THE ECONOMY TO FINANCE

We believe we have demonstrated that, in our financial system, the Economy—the nutritive and digestive system of a Culture—and its two main auxiliaries, Labor and the Machine, are completely prostituted to Finance. In the immediate sense, to "National" Finance; in the medium term—but also, inevitably—to International Finance.

In this damned system, the power that banks wield through their functions of inventing, developing, buying, selling, regulating, increasing, decreasing, and destroying Money is tremendous. In an era in which, moreover, the most unbridled and crude Materialism prevails, such power is practically absolute. International Finance owns Gold, and since Money is based on it, it owns Money; by owning Money, it possesses Power. The power to elevate any political mediocrity to the summit, raised on a pedestal of money that will finance their election campaign; the power to bring them down, by withdrawing its support, when it suits them. The power to influence, and even more so, to determine, the editorial line of the major news media, which are nothing but a business thanks to advertising, the bastard sister of a natural and legitimate economy. In a word, a total and absolute power: THE POWER, of which the most tyrannical autocrats. Power, in short, that is all the more fearsome and despotic for the community because, precisely because its holders are unknown to the Great Majority, it is unaccountable.

Summarizing what has been said in previous sections, we see that the "modus operandi" of what we call the Theft of the Centuries manifests itself through the following eight steps:

1) Employers' profits and full employment for workers depend on the price level.

2) The price level depends on the amount of money in circulation...

3) The amount of money in circulation depends on loans from the " r" private banks.

4) Loans from private banks depend on deposits at the "central"

bank.

5) Deposits in the "central" bank depend on the loans made by that bank to foreign trade.

6) Loans from the "central" bank to foreign trade depend on the movement of gold.

7) The movement of gold depends on foreign exchange rates.

8) Foreign exchange rates depend on the manipulations of international finance[92].

Moral of the story:

The international banker began making promises to pay importers and exporters. His promises to pay caused an outflow of gold. The outflow of gold caused the "central" bank to call in its loans. The "central" bank's call-in of loans caused private banks to call in theirs. The cancellation of private bank loans caused prices to collapse. The collapse of prices led to a collapse in profits. The collapse of profits resulted in lower wages and, in many cases, worker unemployment. And then...

Then the country was able to produce more cheaply, and the international banker did not have to fulfill his promises to pay, giving real money for them after all. And so, when normality returned—after millions of his fellow citizens had been ruined—he was able to obtain a fifteen percent interest rate on the loan of new promises to pay in the Republic of Monomotapa. Which is quite fine, considering that the whole scheme was carried out with other people's money and that, in a sane world, he would be a poor devil with empty pockets. Instead, he is the holder of an irresponsible power; presidents and sovereigns are puppets he manipulates according to the designs of a deranged millennial policy. He and his ilk— —have managed to prostitute the World Economy. That prostitution takes place in the Brothel of Lies:

The lie that a man who has promised to pay ten times more

[92] A very recent example is the dramatic drop in the price of gold caused by a massive sale of gold bullion on the New York Stock Exchange. As a result, South Africa, with its booming economy, is effectively forced to devalue its currency. Elsewhere, we discuss this and other similar cases of currency manipulation through coordinated actions by high finance.

money than he possesses will be able to keep his promise.

The lie that a loss of gold is disastrous.

The lie that foreign exchange rates must remain fixed and be altered only when "central" banks decide to do so.

The lie that a country lives, above all, thanks to its export trade.

The lie that high purchasing power in the domestic market is harmful because it can hurt export market prices.

The lie that high wages are a threat to that foreign market.

The lie that a country that does not export more than it imports is living beyond its means.

The lie that the remedy for overproduction consists of destroying crops, sabotaging machinery, and workers' strikes.

The lie that money is a commodity and not an instrument of measurement and exchange.

And, at the apex of that pyramid of lies, as the logical culmination of the false premises on which it rests, the Lie that a man, a community, a country, an entire world, can be ruined by having worked too hard, while Hunger begins to make its appearance when stocks of all kinds of goods have reached their highest point.

Behold the magical result of International Capitalism: general demoralization; the destruction of savings; the proletarianization of the middle classes ; collective indebtedness; savage tax pressure; the discrediting of the concept of Work and the secular canonization of the "clever ones"; the anonymous tyranny of a rabble of undesirables; and the gradual suppression of all freedoms in the name of a theoretical Freedom devoid of any substance. That path of calamities leads, inevitably, to the Paradise on Earth offered by Satan: to State Capitalism, the misnamed "Communism," the false opposite of Capitalism, and in reality its natural offspring.

THE SYSTEM

THE FORERUNNERS

The famous English Catholic writer, Gilbert Keith Chesterton, wrote that "the characteristic of modern government is that one does not know who actually governs. We see the professional politician, but not the one who backs him; even less the one who backs the backer, nor—what is far more important—the banker of the backer... Enthroned above us all with incredible firmness is the hidden prophet of finance, governing the lives of men and casting exorcisms in a language unknown to all. The press speaks at length of the hardships of the Russians under Soviet power. The newspapers ask with indignation where communist money comes from. But is there anyone who knows where any money comes from?"[93].

And another Englishman, a Protestant, Brailsford, maintained that: "Finance is the true sovereign and arbiter of the modern economy. It is the only autocracy that survives in our time. It produces the ebbs and flows of commerce, just as the Moon governs the tides. It regulates business and rations jobs"[94].

In the study we have conducted on the current global economic chaos, under the overarching title of Misery in Abundance, we have repeatedly referred to International Finance. We consider it necessary, within the framework we have outlined, to explain, at the very least, the composition, means, procedures, and purposes of Finance—or, as it is beginning to be called in "insider" circles, the System. The System that creates Money, as Chesterton suggested, and regulates our lives, as Blailsford clearly denounced.

* * *

While it is true that the Phoenicians were the precursors of the

[93] Gilbert K. Chesterton: "*England's Little History*".

[94] Hector N. Brailsford: "Finance"

banking system, it is no less true that the main activity of those remarkable seafarers of Antiquity was pure and simple, un d trade. Usury—defined here as the lending of money at interest—appeared in Greece, where it was legalized by the Constitutions of the Athenian lawgiver Solon. Plato, however, had already denounced the notion of making money beget money as an aberration against nature. Babylon and Rome also practiced complex banking systems, with their usual culmination: usury. In Republican Rome, the usurer Verres became famous, the target of Cicero's satires.

It was Christianity that outright banned usury, or lending at interest, and under Emperor Constantine, usurers could face penalties ranging from ten years in the galleys to death. With the collapse of the Western Roman Empire, the banking system virtually disappeared, although moneylenders and lenders continued to exist, facing severe penalties when discovered by the authorities. The Roman Pontiffs issued numerous papal bulls and edicts against usurers, and as a result, in those times of pure faith, Christians withdrew entirely from the money trade, leaving the field open to the Jews. From the 9th century onward, says Henry Coston[95], Jews were the only moneylenders in the West. "Specialists in secured lending, Jews would be the only ones to practice it in the West for five centuries. They would establish the rules of this business, drawing inspiration both from the religious precepts of the Talmud and from the practical necessities of the trade"[96]. This inevitably led to numerous hardships for them. The popes issued a barrage of condemnations against them, with a rigor and harshness of language that Dr. Goebbels would never have dared to use in his day. Despite the repression they suffered, they always returned to the fray with the typical tenacity of their race. When a benevolent and weak monarch, such as Charles the Bald of France, abolished certain measures that hindered the activities of the Lords of Money, they gave free rein to their nature and attained a position of privilege; it is no longer enough for them that in the then ultra-Catholic France they are tolerated in the free exercise of their religion, but rather it is necessary for the monarch to order that French merchants not work on the Sabbath and that the courts not summon them to trial on that day. Such audacity provoked general outrage, but they had completely won the trust of the

---

[95] Henry Coston: "*Les Financiers qui mènent le monde,*" p. 17.

[96] A. Dauphin-Meunier: "*History of the Bank,*" p. 23.

unfortunate Charles the Bald, who would eventually die poisoned by a Jew, Sedecio. The power of the Jews in the major kingdoms of Christendom was immense— —but disorganized. Such power—the transformation of Money into Power is an alchemy that this remarkable people has always practiced with marvelous skill—is exercised individually, and for equally individual ends. It will not be until the nineteenth century that the political-financial activities of Judaism transcend individual, family, or, at most, national boundaries, and become international.

Despite popular revulsion, Jews manage to attain positions of influence. They are tax collectors on behalf of the monarchs and of the "dénier de Saint Pierre" (St. Peter's denarius) on behalf of the Roman pontiffs. They are, as Michelet says, "the indispensable intermediary between the Treasury and the victim of the Treasury, taking money from those below to hand it over to kings and the powerful with a repugnant smirk"[97]. But in all this back-and-forth, they always kept some money for themselves, until they eventually became the wealthiest people in every country, without ever having engaged in any productive trade.

Their very power was the cause of envy among the powerful, who were also annoyed by the constant complaints of their subjects. And so, Philip IV expelled them from France in 1306, confiscating all their assets. The same monarch, convinced that the famous Order of the Templars had been infiltrated by numerous Jews, dissolved it, burning its Grand Master, convicted of heresy. The Templars had become renowned moneylenders, and while it is true that they financed several Crusades, it is no less true that they also aided the Muslims and, in secret, practiced demonolatry[98]. Shortly before, the Jews had been expelled from England by King Edward the Confessor, also because of their usurious practices. The same occurred in Naples, Hungary, and numerous Germanic states. Aside from these general, official measures enacted by Christian states, led by the Papal States themselves, uncontrolled popular reactions against moneylenders were widespread

[97] Jules Michelet: *"Histoire de France"*.

[98] The Judaization of the Templar Order cannot be seriously disputed, nor can the fact that they secretly worshipped the Great Baphomet, a semi-animal, semi-human representation of the Devil. In Freemasonry, where there is so much that is Jewish, a good part of the Templar ritual is found.

everywhere, from Poland and Russia (the Russian term "pogrom," or massacre of Jews, has entered all languages) to Spain, where, in 1491, in Barcelona, the army had to intervene to prevent the collective murder of the entire Jewish community. A year later, the Jews were expelled from Spain, and although the official reason was their non-affiliation with the Catholic religion, it would be naive to deny that the usurious practices of that community had much to do with such a drastic measure.

But if that astonishing people were expelled from one country, they soon appeared in another. With incredible tenacity, with a gregarious capacity for masochism, they settled in other lands, arousing the compassion of the simple folk, while—as masters of flattery—they befriended the powerful. After a certain time, their "commercial" practices earned them general antipathy. Princes and sovereigns tolerated them for a while longer, due to their usefulness as ruthless tax collectors, but eventually yielded to pressure from the common people, and once again the persecutions and expulsions returned. Linked to the usurious rationale behind these events is the religious rationale. "In the Middle Ages," says Michelet[99], "the owner of gold is the Jew, that unclean man who cannot touch a woman or a commodity without them being burned; the disgusting deicide whom everyone spits upon..."

These persecutions, these mutual abuses, were, in reality, inevitable. The Jew and the Westerner belong to different Cultures, understanding Culture as the superior organic being that embodies a unity of Nation-State-Race-Destiny[100]. The territorial coexistence of two Cultures is radically impossible, and even more so when dealing with totally antagonistic Cultures, as in the case at hand. "Goodwill," "tolerance," and other such humanitarian nonsense are of no use. Life has its own laws, and one of them pertains to the territorial domain of lower animals, higher animals (sometimes not so much), and Cultures. The territorial coexistence of two Cultures can only engender war between them. And living beings wage war with their own weapons. The Westerner, openly. The Great Parasite, treacherously, by the imperative of its own nature.

---

[99] Jules Michelet: "*History of France*."

[100] Francis Parker Yockey: "*Imperium*," Omnia Veritas Ltd.

We have deemed the preceding paragraph absolutely essential, because the solution to the problems of the West depends on its complete understanding; not merely the purely economic problems, but the political ones—that is, the totality of them: racial, geographical, cultural, military, and, ultimately—but also with a vital, character—economic.

It has precisely been a typical characteristic of the Jewish People to always return to the places from which they have been expelled. And when they have not returned as Jews, they have done so by adopting the ethnic designation of other peoples who have temporarily served as their hosts. Thus, shortly after being expelled from France as Jews, they reappeared as "Lombards." In reality, Lombard moneylenders—authentic Lombards—had already existed in France since 1210, attracted by the Counts of Champagne, and acted as treasury bankers and tax collectors. Following the official expulsion of the Jews, a "Lombard"—who was actually Jewish—Musciatto degli Franzesi, managed the finances of Philip IV, assisted by his brother Biccio. Another disguise they adopted was that of the "Cahorsins," who, although they believed themselves to be from Cahors in central France, actually came from Cuorsa in Piedmont.

The "Cahorsin" moneylenders aided both sides during the Albigensian Crusade. Simon de Montfort granted the "Cahorsin" Raymond de Salvagnac the right to plunder the town of Lavaur as interest. And the "Lombard" Jacques (or Jacob) Jean was given the city of Provins as interest. In general, both the "Lombards" and the "Cahorsins" lent to individuals at interest rates that never fell below 23 percent per year. In Nîmes and Beaucaire, 50 percent and sometimes 100 percent[101]. The activities of these moneylenders naturally made them unpopular, although the protection of the popes, especially Gregory IX and Innocent IV, spared them many problems. Papal protection was based on the fact that the "Lombards" were the collectors of the "Denarius of St. Peter," a tax collected directly by the Papal States throughout the Christian world, which could amount to as much as ten percent of the nobles' income and fifteen percent of the peasants'. But the "Lombards" also lost Vatican protection when Innocent IV realized that they were keeping a portion of the collected funds far greater than what was stipulated. And so Charles VI once

---

[101] Henry Coston: *"The Financiers Who Rule the World,"* p. 29.

again expelled the Jews, "Cahorsins," "Lombards," or whatever they were called.

The "Cahorsins" returned to Italy and North Africa. And the "Lombards" went to England, as we have already mentioned at under the heading "Central Banks." There they joined other Jews who had been expelled from Milan almost simultaneously, also because of their usurious practices, and both groups set themselves up as moneylenders, lending money at ten percent interest.

Gradually, the first "financiers" began to appear, getting involved in politics. Jacques Coeur, a mysterious figure born in Bordeaux in the early 16th century, is the first financier mentioned in French history. Despite having been convicted of counterfeiting, Charles VII entrusted him with the Kingdom's finances, based in the capital of Bourges. He soon amassed a colossal fortune and, at the same time, enormous influence. He rose to become General Counselor of the Kingdom, while his brother was consecrated bishop of Luçon and his son archbishop of Bourges. The Pope used him for confidential diplomatic missions. His rapid rise created numerous enemies, and he was accused of poisoning Agnés Sorel, Charles VII's favorite. During the trial, new charges were brought against him: heretical practices, the sale of Christians as slaves in the East, and the protection of "Lombard" usurers, among others. Sentenced to a modest fine, he chose to go to prison rather than pay, but soon escaped thanks to rare acts of complicity, eventually ending his days in Rome, where Pope Callixtus III took him under his protection.

The Medici of Florence, bankers to Popes John XXII and Martin V, were the Italian counterparts of the rapacious and brilliant Jacques Coeur. The Medici were "transitional figures between the money merchants of the Middle Ages and the bankers of modern times"[102], skillfully dealing in money, with all the honesty that the "trade" allows, managing all the movement of funds necessary for the holding of the Council of Constance, from 1414 to 1418, and later, in 1431, that of Basel, the Medici attained a political and financial prominence unparalleled until then. Above all, Lorenzo de' Medici, nicknamed "the Magnificent," brought legendary splendor to his banking house, but subordinated the conduct of his financial operations to high politics, participating in nearly all the major international intrigues of his time.

---

[102] A. Dauphin-Meunier: *"Histoire de la Banque,"* p. 67.

Upon his death, despite the protection of Pope Innocent VIII, the house began to decline. Although the name of the Medici, the first great Christian financiers, would survive, the house would quickly disappear as a financial and political center. The Medici can be considered a precursor to the Morgans and Cyrus Eaton, "gentile" bankers who actively collaborated with Jewish colleagues and were, gradually, absorbed or supplanted by them. Those who eclipsed the Medici, in their time, were the Fuggers.

The Fuggers, from Augsburg, were as powerful as or more powerful than the Medici, but much more discreet. Hans Fugger, a Christian weaver, married a Jewish woman, and the couple's eldest son, Jacob, who became head of the Augsburg weavers' guild, devoted himself to moneylending. The couple had five sons, all of whom married Jewish women, but only two followed in their father's footsteps: Mark and Jacob. The Fuggers maintained financial ties with the Papacy and the Habsburg dynasty. Jacob Fugger II became banker to the Holy Roman Empire. In 1519, he provided the funds necessary to buy the votes of the Electors who elevated Maximilian's nephew, Charles V of Germany, to the imperial throne, who would later also occupy the throne of Spain. This Fugger wrote to Emperor Charles in 1523 in the following terms: "It is known and evident that Your Majesty would not have obtained the Imperial Crown without me"[103]. The Fuggers charged extremely low interest rates (1 percent) when dealing with private individuals, but their business strategy consisted of lending money to public authorities on favorable terms: in exchange, these authorities granted them the right to exploit mines, as well as favors and privileges. Thus they gained control of the copper and silver mines of Tyrol and Hungary; of mercury in Spain (Almadén), as well as vast mining regions in Venezuela. A branch of the Fuggers settled in Spain, changing their surname to the Hispanicized form of Fúcar. Antonio Fúcar financed Philip II of Spain's war against France and against the Turks. The Fugger-Fúcars were already bankers to the Holy See when they were entrusted with the right to mint the currency of the Papal States, and, disregarding their former alliance with the Medici, they gradually wrested all their positions from them. But the Decree of Valladolid in 1557, by which Philip II suspended payment of all his debts and prohibited the export of Spanish gold, brought about the ruin

[103] A. Dauphin-Meunier: "*History of the Bank,*" p. 69.

of the Fuggers.

The last great “independent” financier, whose activities would foreshadow those of modern finance, was Samuel Bernard, a Huguenot by religion but, according to Voltaire and Drummont, Jewish by race. Regarded as the Croesus of his time, Bernard, banker to Louis XV and of France, used his economic power to extract concessions from the monarch in favor of his co-religionists who, despite renewed prohibitions, kept returning to settle in that country. His vast fortune, the fact that he enjoyed royal favor, and his influence in European society prompted noble and powerful families to seek alliances with his wealthy descendants. The Clermont-Tonnerres, the Cossé-Brissacs, and the Saint-Chamans were able to restore luster to their coats of arms thanks to the inheritance of the financier Samuel Bernard. One of the descendants of that alliance between Money and the Nobility, Mathieu-François Molé, was commissioned by Napoleon to preside over the deliberations of the Grand Sanhedrin in 1807—an event that occurred for the first time and paved the way for the formal recognition of a Jewish nation within France, something the Great Corsican would soon come to regret.

THE BREEDING GROUND

By the very momentum of events, and because of their common interests, the financial dynasties gradually grouped together, and in certain cases merged, until they formed what is commonly called International Finance, and what the "initiates" call the System, or in English, the Establishment.

But to bring about, to realize what Treitschke called "grand politics," Money alone is not enough. Money is not sufficient, on its own, even to carry out a financial policy. Even for something as concrete and material as Finance, a guiding spirit, a soul—[104] —is needed. We have already noted that the "modus operandi" of the precursors of Finance consisted of the trade in money and, through it, the trafficking of influence. But by transforming the once-honorable banking business—which consisted of safeguarding the public's savings in exchange for a fee—into the prodigious scam we have already examined in detail, the possibilities for financiers reached limits unimaginable even to the elites, and certainly completely unbelievable to the general public. It was no longer a matter of lending money, but of inventing it, of creating it out of thin air. To do so, they had to overcome government opposition, for no monarch, no healthy republic, would ever agree that the measurement and exchange of a country's goods should depend on the whims of private individuals or institutions—or, in any case, of outsiders alien to the national interest. Hence, what is generically called "the Revolution"—from the bourgeois French Revolution to the "communist" Russian Revolution, through the endless series of anarchist, "socialist," democratic, and other utopias—has always enjoyed the decisive support of High Finance. The writer Anatole France, whose republicanism cannot legitimately be doubted, stated: "One of the benefits of our Revolution has been to hand France, bound hand and foot, over to the men of Money, who have been devouring it for a hundred years"[105]. And Pierre Gaxotte, undoubtedly the foremost historian specializing in the French Revolution, did not hesitate to say

---

[104]Mario Alberti: "*The Body and Soul of Money*," Rome 1935.

[105] Anatole France: "*The Red* Lily"

that: "Without the massive and brazen support of the international powers of Money, occasionally led by England, the phenomenon known as the French Revolution would never have occurred"[106].

The Finance-Revolution conclusion, about which so much has been written, is so evident that it seems impossible that it is fully understood and accepted by only a few. The only explanation we find lies in the generally forgotten phenomenon of human mental laziness. "Some men," says Bernard Shaw, "would rather die than think. They are the martyrs of human stupidity"[107]. Of course, due credit must be given to school history textbooks, according to which the French and Russian Revolutions—those of Liberty and Equality—occurred because the hungry and exploited people rose up against the tyranny of the wealthy classes... when the reality is that the France of Louis XVI, though indebted due to the disastrous policies of Law and Necker, possessed, if we are to speak in accounting terms, assets far exceeding its liabilities, and its working classes enjoyed the highest standard of living in Europe at the time, while Nicholas II's Russia, despite its backwardness relative to the West, had achieved a per capita income unmatched until then… and since then. This complicity between capitalists and revolutionaries is not only historically true but necessary. Indeed, to organize a "spontaneous" revolution, one must:

a) Hire—and pay—professional actors and agitators, who, with their inflammatory speeches, will convince a majority of fools that they are deeply unhappy and that the established powers exploit them. It is a psychological axiom that for every mediocre person willing to admit their own mediocrity, there will be a hundred willing to blame "Society"—that is, everyone else.

b) Hire—and pay for—the rental of the venues where the agitators' rallies will take place.

c) Hire—and pay—the "thugs" tasked with maintaining order in those halls, and "convince" dissenters with their fists.

d) Hire—and pay—second-rate scribblers, doctors without patients, lawyers without cases, and, in general, the rabble of failed professionals, to draft the revolutionary pamphlets that must be printed, distributed, and posted on walls.

---

[106] Pierre Gaxotte: "*The French Revolution*".

[107] G. Bernard Shaw: "*The Apple Cart.*"

e) Hire—and pay—the printers, typesetters, necessary for such a task.

f) Hire—and pay for—ad space in various media outlets.

g) Hire—and pay—teams of self-sacrificing revolutionaries whose mission will be to disrupt public order. Such disruptions of order, which tend to occur with remarkable synchronization, cannot, under any circumstances, result from "spontaneous" actions.

h) Hire—and pay—teams of lawyers whose sole mission will be to provide legal assistance to revolutionaries detained by the police.

i) Hire—and pay for—supplies of caches of handguns and oth[108] s necessary for street revolutionary action.

j) Hire—and pay—the services of traitors in the Army, the Police, and the Administration, without whom no revolution has ever succeeded.

To organize a Revolution, one must contract—and pay for—so many things that it remains within the reach only of exceptionally wealthy groups. This is the case now; this has always been the case, and it can never be any other way.

This necessary capitalist-revolutionary collusion has had its inevitable parallels throughout history. For it is historically irrefutable that the relatively peaceful English Revolution, which ended with the execution of King Charles I and the establishment of Cromwell's dictatorship, received powerful support from the Sephardic bankers of Amsterdam and those recently expelled from Spain, as well as from the "Lombards" settled in London. The spectacular result, of course, was the establishment of the House of Commons, and the decisive step for Finance—and, ultimately, for Intra-History—the legalization of usury and the subsequent creation of the so-called Bank of England.

The same can be said of the French Revolution. The attack by International Finance against the last three kings of the Capetian dynasty was of a violence unknown until then. A Scottish- n adventurer, John Law, who, according to Gaxotte[109], was an agent of Fernández Carbajal—the Sephardic banker behind Cromwell's triumph and the

[108] Sometimes, not so "short." The glorious Red Army, during the October Revolution in Russia, even had tanks and cannons, which we frankly doubt were purchased with the dues of Party members.

[109] Pierre Gaxotte: Ibid. Id. Op. cit.

creation of the Bank of England—settled in Paris and offered his services to Louis XIV, who rejected them. He then came into contact with the Duke of Orléans, the monarch's cousin and pretender to the French Crown. Louis XIV ordered Law's expulsion[110] but Law returned to France after the king's death. He founded a private bank, and later a West India Trading Company, whose capital was entirely underwritten by the Law Bank. This new company obtained the royal privilege of exclusive trade with Louisiana, the Americas, the Indies, China, and Africa. A year and a half later, a royal edict transformed the Law Bank into the "Royal Bank." That bank implemented the credit system, but with little prudence, which led to its bankruptcy after two years. The state was forced to grant a moratorium, going into debt itself to prevent the ruin of thousands of account holders, while Law fled to England to escape the arrest warrant issued against him.

"But," says Henry Coston, "the money manipulators took their revenge in 1789. Taking advantage of the revolution that swept away the throne of Saint Louis, they established a shameful dominion over the ruins of old France, especially if we consider that it was exercised, in the name of the French people, by men generally alien to their customs, their traditions, and their faith"[111].

Much has been said about the role of the encyclopedists and conspirators in the gestation of the French Revolution. Less has been said, though his importance was paramount, of the Swiss financier Necker. The son of a Prussian lawyer residing in Geneva, Necker very early on entered the service of the Isaac Vernet Bank. Initially a Lutheran, he converted to Calvinism and joined Freemasonry. Isaac Vernet appointed him director of his Paris branch. "Having bribed a high-ranking official in the Ministry of Foreign Affairs, Necker learned of the secret peace negotiations between France and England. He bought up all the English securities he could find on the market at a bargain price and, after the Treaty of Paris in February 1763, resold them for a profit of 1,800,000 pounds"[112]. A similar operation, this time

---

[110] Henry Coston states in "*La Haute Banque et les* Trusts" that Law's real surname was Lasse, and that he was certainly neither Scottish nor English.

[111] Henry Coston: "*Les* financiers..." p. 29.

[112] Jacques Bordiot: "*Une main cachée* dirige..." p. 65.

based on Canadian debts, made him the wealthiest man in the kingdom.

Yielding to multiple pressures from his "entourage," Louis XVI summoned Necker and tasked him with bringing order to the country's finances. For a few months, Necker seemed to be the panacea. To restore the Public Treasury, all he did was issue loans, borrowing money at scandalous interest rates. In four years, he tripled the country's debt; his policy, supported primarily by foreign bankers such as the Genevans Hottinguer, Mallet, Mirabaud, Vernes, and, above all, Isaac Vernet, was based on multiplying the debt "ad infinitum." Furthermore, he constantly pressured the King to grant authorization for the establishment of a "Central Bank," like those already operating in Holland and England. His protection of certain revolutionaries was the cause—along with his misguided economic policy—of his dismissal by the King. But pressure from the "Societies of Thought" forced the weak Louis XVI to recall him in 1788, that is, seven years after his dismissal. Necker's return sparked extravagant displays of enthusiasm from a "public opinion" that had been conveniently manipulated. On December 27, 1788, in his report to the Royal Council, Necker, without any restraint, attacked Louis XVI and his prime minister, Vergennes, the "bête noire" of the revolutionaries. Six months later, in May 1789, the Estates-General was convened, the embryo of the future Parliament, a goal for which the millionaire financier Necker had fought for years. Two months later, the indecisive Louis XVI dismissed Necker once again. It was July 11. New unrest among the Parisian populace in support of Necker. Street riots and the storming of the Bastille on the 14th, and the following day, the unfortunate Louis XVI, compelled by "Brother" General Lafayette, recalled Necker. In 1790, with the country completely ruined and the monarch practically a prisoner of the revolutionaries—who would guillotine him three years later—Necker, completely discredited by those who had supported him despite his vacuity and abandoned him when he was no longer needed, returned to Geneva, alongside his mentor Isaac Vernet.

* * *

We have previously referred to the "Sociétés de Pensée" or Societies of Thought, which were nothing more than Masonic lodges that allowed occasional attendance by sympathizers who were not members of the Sect. The influence of these "Societies" on the outbreak of the French Revolution was of paramount importance. This is not the appropriate place to delve into a detailed account of Freemasonry's centuries-long struggle against the Crown of Saint Louis until its downfall in the French Revolution. Authors of the stature of Bernard Fay, Augustin Cochin, Copin-Albancelli, Gustave Bord, Gaston Martin, Henry Coston, Georges Virebeau, and the Englishwoman Nesta H. Webster have addressed the subject in depth and with exhaustive documentation. In reality, Freemasonry has been, and remains, an enemy of all thrones, even though for tactical reasons it has at times supported others, or tolerated the existence of certain thrones, especially when dealing with merely symbolic thrones—that is, those devoid of actual authority.

But what we wish to mention specifically here is that Freemasonry, together with the Revolution[113], is one of the components of the System's breeding ground. The third component is International Finance. We repeat: International Finance, for all its omnipotence, is nothing more than one component among others. Finance is a tool, just as Communism is, just as Anarchism was, just as Trotskyism nearly became, and just as the anti-racist Racism of people of color may become tomorrow.

But there is more to it. The System is more than that. The System is what is known as Globalism, represented by the nefarious United Nations and the mysterious groups of individuals who, in a highly undemocratic manner, are appointed through co-optation, such as the Bilderberg Group, which we will discuss later. The System, in short, is nothing more than the fulfillment of old messianic prophecies; it is, no more and no less, a sprawling organization whose ultimate goal—whether all or most of its members are aware of it or not—is world domination.

---

[113] We refer to the Revolution in accordance with the meaning most people give to the word, and not to the concept evoked by its etymological meaning.

NAPOLEON AND ROTHSCHILD

If Necker had left the state coffers empty, a host of political hacks—among whom those born outside France abounded, such as the Prussian Jew Anacharsis Klotz, the Sephardic Chocerlos de Laclos, the also Sephardic Almereyda (Portuguese) and Guzmán (Spanish), and, above all, the bloodthirsty Jew Jean Paul Marat, imposed the Terror—blind and arbitrary—as a form of government, relying on the rabble of the great cities. From that rabble had emerged what Spengler called "the negative elite of the gutter," the abysmal world of the inferior, the resentful, the failures; professionals without a profession; dreamers, idlers, and drunkards; prostitutes, charlatans, and demagogues; the physically and morally retarded; inferior beings who hated Society and established values, precisely because of their own inferiority. People who, under the guise of the famous triad of Liberty-Equality-Fraternity, made a fortune. All of them, in the end, perpetrators and victims, in turn, of the dynamics of Evil; of the principle according to which Evil is evil even to Evil itself. In short, all in the service of anti-national, cosmopolitan forces, as they were already called back then. In the trial of the "Hébertists," for example, it was demonstrated that they were all as anti-French as they were anti-democratic, as they accused one another without the slightest restraint. They were guillotined as accomplices of the "Foreign Power": the Judeo-Prussian Klotz; Danton, the illustrious stipend-holder of England—or, more precisely, of the Bank of England; the Sephardic Guzmán; the Austrian Jewish bankers Emmanuel and Junius Frey; Madame de Haelder, agent of the King of Prussia and founder of the Masonic "Fraternal Society of the Two Sexes," of which the Dutch adventuress and spy Etta Palm was a member—an agent of the Bank of Amsterdam and mistress of the deputy Choudieu, an agent of the Netherlands[114]. But, months later, the "Jacobins," executors of the "Hébertists," would, in turn, go to the guillotine.

The wars of the Directory—writes Henry Coston[115] —allowed the

[114] Jacques Bordiot: *"Une main cachée dirige...,"* p. 83.

[115] Henry Coston: *"Les* Financiers..." p. 51.

financiers, who had become masters of the state, to exploit the conquests carried out by the generals. In 1799, the ruined Directory learned that "its" banker, Ouvrard, had refused to supply it with more money. The government then announced measures against the "speculative" financiers. The bankers were alarmed and sought a sword to impose order on that chaos. The bankers Perregaux and Marmot recalled a certain General Bonaparte who, in Egypt, as previously in Italy, had proven himself not only a great strategist but also a prudent administrator of the conquered territories. Perregaux and Marmont sent their emissary Bourbaki to Egypt, who informed Bonaparte that "two million francs were at his disposal in anticipation of a coup d'état"[116]. Leaving his troops under the command of General Kléber, Napoleon hurried to Paris, where the bankers Le Couteulx, Perregaux, and Marmot—father of the aide-de-camp to the victor of the Pyramids—were anxiously awaiting him. In reality, High Finance had no interest in overthrowing the Directory, nor could it suspect that Ouvrard, first, and then Perregaux, Le Couteulx, and Marmont, were acting on their own, without consulting the fledgling but increasingly powerful Power of Money, based in London and Amsterdam. That is why the necessary measures were taken to prevent a repeat of the scandalous occurrence of a banker thinking more of his homeland than of the interests of the International Financial System; and this would not happen again until one hundred and thirty years later, in Germany.

But let us not get ahead of ourselves and return to Paris, where the money and influence of Perregaux, Le Couteulx, and Marmont secured the election of Luciano Bonaparte as President of the National Assembly in April 1799. Le Couteulx had himself elected President of the administration of the Seine Department. He bought the complicity of Lemercier, President of the Council of Elders. General Marmont, a key figure in the conspiracy—being the son of a banker, Perregaux's son-in-law, and Bonaparte's aide-de-camp—convinced General Jubé, head of the Directory's Guard, to join the conspirators. Jubé confined the members of the Directory—whose safety had been entrusted to him—in the Luxembourg Palace, while Napoleon had the members of the two Assemblies forcibly taken to the Château de Saint-Cloud and there, under the pretext of saving the Republic, strangled it. On 19 Brumaire (November 11, 1799), Napoleon Bonaparte was named First

[116] A. Dauphin-Meunir: "*La Banque à travers les Âges,*" Vol. II, p. 71.

Consul[117].

Can it be said that, because he owed his power to them, Napoleon was the puppet of a small group of financiers? Absolutely not. On the contrary: for although he showed gratitude toward those who had contributed to his rise to power, he never hesitated, when it served the interests of France or his policies, to stand up to them with all the rigor demanded by the circumstances.

Napoleon, undoubtedly the most exalted figure of an era in which great men abounded, has been described in the most diverse ways and from the most disparate angles by second-rate historians who, at best, have seen in him a fortunate upstart adventurer, versed in military tactics and strategy. But true historians, beginning with the staunchly monarchist Jacques Bainville, have recognized the great statesman, legislator, and economist: the Genius. Napoleon, in the midst of the Italian campaign, had come to the conclusion that what France urgently needed, to put an end once and for all to the chaos orchestrated for the benefit of the Stateless Finance, was a King. He even suggested to Sieyès the possibility of bringing back the Bourbons. Unfortunately, the brother and heir of Louis XVI, who in his London exile called himself Louis XVII, received a pension from the British government and threatened to seek English aid to subdue his "rebellious subjects." Such unworthy conduct, unbecoming of a true monarch, made the Restoration impossible. "The French Nation," said Napoleon, "needs a hereditary leader... I would even recommend the Bourbon Restoration, if they (the Bourbons) had today in Europe any other title of consideration or strength other than that derived from the contemptible salaries they receive from England, or from the financiers who impose their will on that island, and if the French did not have good reason to fear that their return would bring upon their heads the contempt their weakness deserves, and would lead to the destruction of our current institutions at the hands of ignorant people who hate them"[118].

Napoleon judged the French Revolution from the same perspective as Mirabeau, that is, as a means and not as an end. As a means of purging the feudal system of abuses, a system rendered obsolete by Life

---

[117] A. Dauphin-Meunier: *"La Banque à travers les Âges,"* Vol. II, p. 79.

[118] R. Mc Nair Wilson: *"God and the Goldsmiths,"* p. 94.

itself.

Napoleon wished to carry out "the Revolution from above," that is, the only Revolution possible. A Revolution that he was prepared to carry out by restoring the Throne—"a monarch," he said, "cannot be bribed" —which in his mind amounted to dominating the Financial System, which, logically, would fight against the Throne as it had already done in the days of the indecisive Louis XVI. He realized it would be a multifaceted, sprawling struggle. He knew that Money never fights openly, face-to-face, but through agents who often do not even know the objective they serve and, a fortiori, the Forces and men pursuing that objective. Napoleon knew that there was international money behind each of his enemies; it was behind the puppet Louis XVII and the entire monarchist party; it was behind the bloody ultra-revolutionaries of the Jacobin Club; and it was, above all, within the Jewish community of France. One of the first measures taken by the Convention, in fact, was not only to allow the uncontrolled immigration of Jews, but to grant them the enjoyment of all civil rights, even when they had just arrived from a ghetto in Transylvania. The Jews, as always and everywhere, were, individually and collectively, in the service of International Money. They would bring down—relying, as always and everywhere, on the respectable patriotism of other nations or on the treachery of discontented elements within—anyone who dared to oppose the designs of the Great Parasite. The Eagle of Austerlitz, despite having identified his Enemy from the outset and having taken measures, both internal and external, to protect himself from its venomous bites, would ultimately succumb.

Napoleon sought to restore the idea of service, at a time when demagoguery spoke only of "rights." He put a stop to the activities of the bankers; he proclaimed that "credit belongs to the Nation, not to the bankers." At the end of the 18th century, First Consul Bonaparte surveyed an old world in which the system of service was everywhere in melancholic decline. In the declining monarchies, a privileged class viewed the bankers with suspicion, as the bankers coveted their privileges. In England, the gallantry with which George III had begun his reign was fading. The monarch, following his humiliation in America—which we will discuss later—no longer dared to act against the interests of the City of London; that very City which had spectacularly betrayed England in the war with the American colonies would later throw its weight behind England itself against France—or, more precisely, against the Idea of Service and European Messianism that the Great Corsican embodied in those circumstances. McNair Wilson states that "the financiers exported and imported gold without paying the slightest heed to the law or the state of war; their operations escaped any sanction, because those who might have imposed it were associated with their enterprises and reaped formidable profits"[119]. It is an incontrovertible historical truth that, throughout his life, Napoleon sought an alliance with England; he always understood that the English people were one thing and the men of the City another. He never hesitated to proclaim the deep admiration he felt for England and its institutions. On one occasion he told the English ambassador: "Everything would be possible for humanity if France, the leading continental power, and England, the leading naval power, were united." Thus, he proposed a peace treaty to the English government, which was signed in Amiens in late 1799, whereby France, with no other consideration than to demonstrate to London its spirit of goodwill and peace, undertook that its war fleet would in no case exceed one-third of the British fleet in tonnage. Furthermore, Napoleon, who had defeated all his enemies, issued a sweeping amnesty, recalled all those in exile, and, once religion had been restored, attended a solemn Te Deum at Notre Dame.

After making peace with his external enemies, Napoleon sought to bring order to internal affairs. He prohibited, under the severest penalties, the export of money from France and ordered that, under no pretext or circumstance, should borrowing be resorted to in order to cover ordinary civil or military expenses. These measures were intended to prevent bankers from putting the government in a difficult position, as they had already done with Louis XV, Louis XVI, the Convention, and the Directory. When a government is financially dependent on the banking system, the true government is the bankers, since "the hand that gives is above the hand that receives."

As Napoleon himself told his loyal Las Cases, "Money has no homeland: financiers have neither patriotism nor decency; their sole object is profit"[120]. One hundred and thirty years later, the Napoleon of our time asserted something similar, adding that profit was not the

---

[119] R. Mc Nair Wilson: *"The Bankers' Conspiracy."*

[120] Las Cases: *"Memorial of Saint Helena."*

ultimate goal, but rather the Power that it provides.

Napoleon's refusal to accept loans of any kind had caused great concern in the City of London. It must not be forgotten that this was no longer just about France, but about more than half the continent— —where the influence of the victorious French army imposed a natural submission to the directives of Paris. Another measure that stirred the spirits of high finance was the creation of the Bank of France. It must be acknowledged that this Bank of France had been advocated by Necker and, consequently, by the financiers who controlled Necker. But what they desired was a Bank of France like their counterparts in England and Holland—that is, the classic "central bank," a coordinator of private banks, and just as "private" as those banks. And what Napoleon created was a true Bank of France—that is, linked to France, belonging to France, and serving only the interests of France. This institution would create money—that is, issue currency as agricultural and industrial production demanded; this money would be born without the stigma of debt and would be entirely unlinked to gold. Furthermore, Napoleon had himself appointed President for life of the Bank, appearing at the top of the first list of shareholders in the institution, alongside people he trusted implicitly, such as his brother Joseph; his brother-in-law Murat; his daughter-in-law Hortense de Beauharnais; and his loyal aides-de-camp Duroc, Clarke, and Bourienne, as well as his confidant Las Cases. The banker Ouvrard, who openly criticized the policy of the new National Bank, was arrested by order of Napoleon, which further increased the hostility of International Finance.

But the measure that brought the hostility to a fever pitch was the First Consul's attitude toward the Jews. If it was Napoleon who ordered the convening of the Grand Sanhedrin of France, his idea was, as his subsequent actions would demonstrate, "to see his Jews," according to Edouard Drumont's phrase[121]. In this, the sure instinct of his marvelous genius did not betray him, for, as Drumont rightly states, "every Jew who is seen, every Jew who is discovered, is relatively harmless, and may even be useful if employed in dishonorable deeds that no one else would agree to carry out. The dangerous Jew is the vagrant Jew, a socialist in word, an agent provocateur, generally in the service of

[121] E. Drumont: "*Jewish France,*" p. 254.

foreign powers, whom he will also betray when it suits him..."[122].

To "see" his Jews, Napoleon demanded, to begin with, that they adopt fixed first and last names, under penalty of expulsion; he forced them to register; he established a "numerus clausus" that affected both their places of residence and certain activities; and he strictly forbade them from engaging in usury. Furthermore, considering that they were too numerous in Alsace and were causing complaints from the region's inhabitants, he ordered the expulsion of more than half of them, sending them to the Vendée, "as punishment for that region, guilty of rebellion in favor of the so-called Louis XVII." But, aside from all these measures, what was evident was the First Consul's animosity. It is said that at a meeting of the Council of State, Napoleon remarked: "No one complains about Catholics or Protestants as they complain about Jews, which proves that this is not a matter of religion, but of race. The harm done by the Jews does not stem from individuals, but from the very idiosyncrasy of that strange people. They are vermin, parasites who want to ruin my France"[123].

And, to add insult to injury for International Finance—which had made the French Revolution possible—the Corsican general Napoleon Bonaparte, who never lost his Corsican accent, proclaimed himself Emperor. He insisted that the Church consecrate him by the hand of the Pope himself, Pius VII, but so that it could not even be surmised that the appointment from Heaven came indirectly through the Church, he placed the Crown of France upon his own head. Napoleon, therefore, was sovereign of France by the Grace of God, with no distinction to be drawn between his sovereignty and that of any other sovereign. "Power comes from God and the People," Napoleon asserted, "but legitimacy does not necessarily derive from inheritance, especially if the heirs have proven themselves unworthy."

Thus, International Finance would organize from London, with ample continental complicity, coalition after coalition against the Great Corsican. Despite having nipped the Jacobins' hysterical anti-Catholic abuses in the bud, Napoleon also faced the barely veiled hostility, if not of the Church as an institution, then at least of the High Clergy, which

---

[122] Ibid. Id. Op. cit., p. 256.

[123] Ibid. Id. Op. cit., p. 259.

never forgave him for his attitude on the day of his coronation as Emperor.

The historian D'Ivernois, hardly suspected of Bonapartism, asserts that it was the High Bank that was to blame for the failure of the continental blockade imposed by Napoleon on England[124], and, consequently, for the forced exile of the Eagle to Saint Helena[125].

Napoleon's fall represented a return to "order," that is, to the reinstatement of usury as the economic-political system for governing the peoples. It also represented a setback for the great Idea of a European Nation embodied by the Genius of the 19th century, which would have meant, within the economic sphere at hand, the creation of an autarkic, economically self-sufficient territorial entity stretching from the Atlantic to the eastern shores of the Baltic, at the very least. Instead, our continent was "balkanized" into an endless array of more or less independent states, although in practice they all depended—whether they knew it or not, and increasingly so—on the omnipotent power of international finance.

But, moreover, chronologically, Napoleon's fall coincided with the emergence on the stage of high politics of the new King of Europe: Rothschild.

Mayer Amschel Rothschild's ancestors lived, like him, in Frankfurt, where they ran a money-lending business against collateral in the ghetto. Since, at first, the Jews did not number the houses in the ghetto's narrow streets, they distinguished one from another by the coat of arms, of a certain color, displayed above the door, or by some other particular emblem. The house inhabited by the members of the Rothschild family was marked by a red coat of arms, and "red shield" translates precisely in German as "Rotes Schild," and this is undoubtedly the origin of the family name "[126]."

Mayer Amschel Rothschild, the true founder of the dynasty, entered

---

124 R. D'Ivernois: *"The Effects of the Continental Blockade."*

125 It is probably a coincidence, but the English governor of Saint Helena, who treated the Emperor so disgracefully, was a Jew named Edmund Lowe.

126 Count Cesare Corti: *"La Maison Rothschild,"* p. 13.

the service of Landgrave Frederick of Hesse-Kassel, the wealthiest prince in the German Confederation, who supplied mercenary soldiers to European sovereigns in need of them. This type of trade was common at the time, and Mayer Amschel was responsible for recruiting the troops, clothing them, housing them, and feeding them until they were sent to their new sovereign. Naturally, he received a handsome commission from Frederick II of Hesse-Kassel, who was the one nominally supplying that "cannon fodder." The French Revolution and the Consulate- an Wars allowed the Elector of Hesse and his high-ranking official Rothschild to do magnificent business. When, in 1806, another coalition was organized against Napoleon, the King of Prussia appealed to the Elector of Hesse for help. He asked him to send soldiers, but admitted that he did not have the money to pay for them. Rothschild advanced the necessary sum, charging exorbitant interest.

In 1810, as he was growing older, Mayer-Amschel brought his five sons into the family business, "Mayer Amschel Rothschild and Sons," assigning them as follows: Nathan Rothschild was sent to London; Salomon, to Paris; James, who was responsible for liaising between the "French" and the "English," would reside in Gravelines, Belgium. His eldest son, Amschel, and Karl would remain with their father in Frankfurt for the time being, although the latter would soon move to Naples. Furthermore, with the disappearance of the House's great enemy, Napoleon, James would move to Vienna, where he would go on to have a formidable career.

The Rothschilds, who reaped enormous profits during the war against Napoleon, further bolstered their fortune with the famous "Waterloo stock market coup." Indeed, having learned from his less-fortunate associates—who, as was the custom of the time, appeared on the battlefield at the end of the battle to finish off the wounded and strip the corpses—that the Emperor had been defeated by the combined forces of Wellington and Blücher, he hurried to London, arriving a day before the news was officially known, spreading the rumor that the Allies had been defeated by Napoleon, thus causing a crash on the London Stock Exchange, while his agents bought up all kinds of securities at rock-bottom prices... which skyrocketed once the truth became known. This move turned the Rothschild millionaires into billionaires[127].

Waterloo, which was more a defeat of the European Ideal than a French defeat, simultaneously marked the rise of a new dynasty: the Rothschild dynasty. From 1815 onward, they became friends and financiers of Louis XVIII, as well as of the Habsburgs of the Austro-Hungarian Empire. The British government even entrusted them with collecting the war reparations that defeated France was required to pay to the victorious English. In 1823, Louis XVIII entrusted them with the issuance of a 414-million-franc loan. Next, Prussia turned to them for assistance, followed by Spain, Naples, Austria-Hungary, the Papal States, and Russia. In 1830, 1831, 1832, and 1834, they negotiated new loans on behalf of the French government. In 1844, they handled another 200-million-franc loan, which caused a scandal, with the Minister of Finance being accused of being in the pocket of the Rothschilds. But suddenly the press in the French capital, evidently bribed, discredited all those who had opposed the Rothschild dynasty and its Minister of Finance.

Numerous volumes have been written about the activities of this astonishing family, both critical and favorable; paradoxically, the latter prove more instructive than the former. The irregularities observed in the operation of the Northern French Railways, in the financing of the Barentin viaduct, which collapsed before it was completed... Meanwhile, in Vienna, Salomon Rothschild was made a baron by the Kaiser and became a personal friend of Chancellor Metternich, at whose side he insidiously placed his agent, a man named Gentz, an Israelite, who informed him of the inner workings of high politics in the powerful Austro-Hungarian Empire. Carlos Rothschild, of Naples, for his part, was received personally by the Pope: he was the first Jew to be granted that honor. Nathan, in London, was the first Jew admitted to the House of Lords[128]. The fortune and, in parallel, the power of the Dynasty rose

---

[127] Eugene de Mirecourt: "Rothschild," p. 64. In contrast, Count Corti, in his work "*La Maison Rothschild,*" states that Nathan did not personally travel from Ostend to Dover due to the storm battering the English Channel, but instead sent his agent Rothworth, a fellow believer, with specific instructions.

[128] In order for Nathan Rothschild to be admitted to the House of Lords, the entire ceremonial had to be modified. Until then, the oath of office was taken using the phrase "... On the good faith of a Christian," which Rothschild refused to do. A fierce controversy erupted, from which money, as is almost always the case, emerged victorious, and since then the English Lords no longer take their oath as "Christians."

ceaselessly. Wars were the harvest of these money traders. In 1835, in Spain, wars broke out over the succession to the throne between liberals and Carlists. Austria-Hungary supported the latter, whose traditionalism appealed to Metternich. England and France aided the Queen Regent and her liberals. The Rothschilds of Vienna, London, and Paris were the conduits for this aid; that is, they lent money, against collateral, to both sides. Thus, the Almadén mines in the south of the Iberian Peninsula—which, along with those at Idria (which the Rothschilds of Vienna had purchased from the Habsburgs), were the only mercury mines on the European continent—passed into the hands of the dynasty, which thereby established, in effect, a monopoly on that metal. And not only that, but the London- n branch of the family established a veritable financial protectorate over the government of the victorious Regent, María Cristina.

At the height of their power, the Rothschilds never forgot their less fortunate co-religionists. The family's interventions with the Holy See, the Austrian government, and the Duke of Modena—whom they forced to rescind certain oppressive measures he had imposed on his Jewish subjects accused of fomenting a revolutionary insurrection—gained great notoriety. But their "bête noire" was Russia; the Tsars, with their anti-Semitic measures, aroused the wrath of the Lords of Gold… and not only of the Rothschilds, but of other influential co-religionists of theirs, such as the Lazards, the Gunzbourgs, and the Reinachs. This would be the cause of their downfall, as we shall see later.

Even the Jewish revolutionaries, such as the wealthy poet Heinrich Heine and the certainly not proletarian Karl Marx, enjoyed Rothschild's protection; Heine, from the German Rothschild, who saved him from going to prison for his support of the revolutionaries; Marx, more discreetly, from the English Rothschild. Money, closely linked to influence peddling, was the foundation of all of Rothschild's politics. Thus, when, in 1848, the Parisian mob—having just proclaimed a "Republic of Labor"—stormed the Tuileries and the Royal Palace, destroying works of art and looting the homes of the wealthy... but the Rothschild house and bank were carefully protected by the police; Caussidière, the Prefect, had been paid to ensure that nothing happened to the "King of the Republic." This designation of "King" applied to Rothschild led to the letters R.F. embroidered on the tricolor flag flying over official buildings—which are the initials of "République Française"—being popularly interpreted as "Rothschild Frères."

If Napoleon III, hostile to the Rothschilds, relied on another Jewish banker, Péreyre—the "little Napoleon," as Victor Hugo called him—he did nothing but go from Scylla to Charybdis; a journey for which no saddlebags were needed. The French government remained under the sway of the financial elite. In any case, the Péreyre Bank, the victim of a conspiracy led by the Rothschilds, would collapse, just as the "Catholic bank" Union Générale would, and Napoleon III would also have to return to the Rothschild fold. They would impose one of their own, Goudchaux, as Minister of Finance, and another, Léon Crémieux, as Minister of Justice. This Crémieux would "distinguish himself" with the absurd measure of granting French nationality en masse to the Jewish population of Algeria, while denying it to the Arabs of that territory. That measure would open a chasm of animosity between the French and the Arabs, as the latter rightly interpreted that decision as humiliating.

The Rothschilds financed the purchase of the Suez Canal shares for England. The Khedive of Egypt had offered them to France, the homeland of Ferdinand de Lesseps, the Canal's founder. But the High Finance, of which the Rothschilds were one of the fundamental pillars, decided that it was in England's interest to control the Canal politically, rather than France's; thus, while the Rothschild in Paris kept the French government occupied with delays based on various pretexts, he informed his relative in London that the Khedive was in a bind and needed to sell his shares. The British Prime Minister, Disraeli[129], appeared before Queen Victoria with an offer from the Rothschild of the City of four million pounds sterling, at a modest interest rate, for the purchase of the Suez Canal shares, which would be swiftly acquired[130]. This came as a real slap in the face to France, but once again money flowed freely among the "press boys," and the matter was quickly buried.

If Rothschild temporarily served England's interests to the detriment of France in the Suez Canal "affair," he would serve Germany's interests—again to the detriment of France—when, at the end of the 1870 war, the "German" banker Bleichroeder and the "French" banker

---

[129] Benjamin Disraeli, Lord Beaconsfield, was a descendant of the Sephardic Jews expelled from Spain by the Catholic Monarchs.

[130] Cesare Corti: "*La Maison Rothschild*," p. 241.

Rothschild literally pulled the wool over the eyes of poor Jules Favre, plenipotentiary of the French government, whom they made sign—presenting it as a diplomatic success—the acknowledgment of war reparations amounting to five billion two hundred million francs[131]. In contrast, at the end of World War I, the Rothschilds and their colleagues in high finance across all countries resolutely turned against Germany, their attitude summed up by the "Frenchman" Simon Klotz, who said: "Le boche payera tout" (The German will pay for everything).

Indeed, one of the cases in which it became most blatantly apparent that high finance, aside from contributing to the creation of pre-war situations, subsequently acted with complete disregard for the interests of the warring parties, occurred during World War I. In 1917, a French senator accused the Rothschilds of selling nickel from New Caledonia, a French colony in Oceania, to Germany through "America Metal Cy," a company that represented the Frankfurt-based "Metallgesellschaft"—a firm controlled

by the Rothschilds of Germany. And in the Reichstag, the German Rothschilds were accused of selling German and Austro-Hungarian wheat to France and England through triangular transactions via neutral countries.

The Rothschilds also intervened in the American Civil War, aiding the Confederate States of the South directly, while supporting the Northerners through their agents, the Belmont bankers, who were their political allies. But it was precisely then that their star would begin to fade. In reality, this is very relative, as the Rothschilds remained at the

---

[131] Alphonse de Rothschild, the "Frenchman," spoke German fluently, but in front of Favre he pretended to know only French, while Bismarck insisted on speaking only German. A scene ensued, very well played, that allowed Rothschild to present himself as a great French patriot. Bismarck was a shrewd man who knew how to use financiers. He was not reckless, as Metternich had been with Salomon de Rothschild. He made use of both Bleichroeder and Rothschild, but asserted: "One must not allow oneself to be influenced by the Jews or place oneself under their financial tutelage, as unfortunately occurs in many countries. Whenever I have to deal with high finance, generally composed of Jews, I am never the one who has to be grateful for anything." And he added: "In dealings with Jews, one must bear in mind that they have a moral code that bears no relation whatsoever to ours. The Jewish scale of values, especially that of Jews engaged in finance, is diametrically opposed to the European scale of values. Anyone who does not fully understand this is lost." (Hermann Hoffmann: "*Prince Bismarck.*" Vol. I, pp. 149–151).

very forefront of the international superpower that High Finance was becoming; however, the emergence of the new political power, the United States of America, caused the center of gravity of Great Politics to gradually shift from Europe to the New Continent, which led to the banking dynasties established there rising to the very highest rank.

Another spectacular intervention by the Rothschilds in politics occurred during the Herzen affair, as recounted by the hardly suspect pen of the Jewish revolutionary Rappoport[132] : "The Bolshevik activist Alexander Herzen was forced to flee Russia, pursued by the Tsarist police, and moved to London, where he began publishing the revolutionary pamphlet 'The Bell.' But before leaving, the wealthy Bolshevik converted his properties into government bonds. The Imperial Government identified the numbers of Herzen's bonds, and when they were presented for payment after Herzen arrived in London, the Tsar, hoping to eliminate his enemy, ordered the State Bank of St. Petersburg not to pay. The Bank obeyed, but the Tsar found himself facing an unexpected enemy, the eldest son of the Rothschilds, who informed him that, since Herzen's bonds were as valid as those of any other Russian, he was obliged to rule on the Imperial Government's insolvency. If the bonds were not paid immediately, he (Rothschild) would declare the Tsar bankrupt, particularly regarding his currency on the European stock exchanges. Nicholas II, stunned, swallowed his pride and paid: The Jews themselves gave this event spectacular publicity, which dealt a severe moral blow to Tsarism.

Today, the Rothschilds remain on the front lines of high finance, behind the Warburgs, the Rockefellers, and the Lehmanns, who, due to their geographic location (America), have managed to stand out from the leading pack of financial dynasties. But the Rothschilds' importance lies in their diabolically clever policy of marriage alliances, which has allowed them to have a foothold in every family within the System. And when the Rothschilds do not appear, their trustees do. Thus, for example, the Aschberg family has controlled the Soviet State Bank since 1917. The Aschbergs, of "Nya Banken" in Stockholm, are regarded as the agents of the Rothschild family in Northern Europe[133]. Another example: in France, following the so-called "Liberation,"

---

[132] Angelo S. Rappoport: "*Pioneers of the Russian Revolution.*"

[133] J. Bochaba: "*Finance and Power,*" Omnia Veritas Ltd.

General Charles de Gaulle emerged as the leading political figure of the Fourth French Republic. De Gaulle had been promoted, from his position as a provisional general, by Spears, an agent of the Rothschilds in London, and throughout his life he followed the political directives of the bankers of Rue Laffitte. But one fine day—a bad day, for him—he had the idea of attacking "that aggressive, proud, and domineering people," referring to the State of Israel. Immediately, the venal French press, evidently "well-funded" by subsidies from Rothschild and Lazard, turned against him, and he was defeated in the elections. But in his place came Pompidou, who, before entering politics, had been General Manager of "Rothschild Frères" in Paris...[134]

[134] Louis Madelin: "*The Revolutionaries.*"

AMERICA, THE NEW PROMISED LAND

The immense possibilities offered by the New Continent were the reason why the interest of the financial world turned toward it.[135] The American War of Independence was, if not fomented, at least encouraged by the Power of Money, which correctly intuited that it would be much easier to control a colonial entity than a leading member of Western civilization, such as England. For this reason, that War represented, chronologically, the first exception to the rule of the traditional alliance between British Imperialism and International Finance; a rule that would remain fully in force for a century, only to gradually fall into disuse, to the point that—whether the English ruling circles realize it or not—it currently functions in a manner entirely contrary to the original.

George III had to literally beg for the money needed to sustain the war against the rebels in the thirteen American colonies—money that was repeatedly withheld from him by a House of Commons dominated by members who were, in turn, agents or front men for the powers of Money. Freemasonry, always aligned with the financial establishment, also this time, unconditionally, on the side of the Americans[136]. Naturally, once the independence of the United States was recognized, Shylock demanded payment of his pound of flesh from his "protégé." Neither Benjamin Franklin's warnings[137] nor the Founding Fathers' legal precautions availed, for in 1791, under the auspices of the Rothschilds of London, the first Bank of the United States was founded.

This Bank was to operate under the same mechanisms as the Bank of England. Prominent figures such as Edmund Randolph, Attorney

---

[135] Culturally, America is a colony of Europe, the Mother of Western Civilization, as demonstrated by Spengler, Treitschke, and Yockey, among other prominent philosophers. A colony lacks sufficient antibodies to combat moral and physical maladies, such as usury and its driving principle, its "soul," materialism.

[136] Arnold S. Leese: "*Gentile Folly*."

[137] "If we do not expel the Jews from this country, within two centuries our descendants will be working for them." Franklin was overly optimistic; it did not take two centuries; barely 125 years were enough.

General of the United States, and Thomas Jefferson, Secretary of State, opposed its establishment. However, it was fervently supported by Alexander Hamilton, one of the Founding Fathers and a famous statesman, who secured the Bank's admission. Hamilton was the son of Rachel Faucett Levine, who was likely Jewish and married to a Danish Jew. Since Jews were not then entitled to American citizenship—even though they could settle freely in America—his mother registered him in the Civil Registry as Alexander Hamilton, claiming that a Scottish sailor of that name was her son's true father. Hamilton was thus the first Jew to obtain American citizenship[138].

After the Bank had been in operation for a few years, Thomas Jefferson said: "I believe that banking institutions are more dangerous to our liberties than hostile armies. They have already formed a banking aristocracy that defies the Government. The power to issue currency should be wrested from the banks and restored to the Government and the People whom it serves." But the "Bank of the United States" continued to thrive, under the ostensible patronage of unquestionably Anglo-Saxon Americans and subject to the "auspices" of the Belmont Jewish bankers, agents of the London Rothschilds in the New World[139]. Indeed, in 1783, the United States of America decided to grant Jews equal civic rights with respect to the Anglo-Saxon-Celtic population that formed the core of the country's population.

The settlement of Jews in North America is one of the episodes that best illustrates the tenacity and ability to adapt to hostile environments that constitute one of the essential characteristics of this remarkable people. The first Jews arrived in America despite the ban imposed by the Governor of New Amsterdam, Peter Stuyvesant. As is well known, the territory on which present-day New York was to be built was initially colonized by the Dutch, who granted the exploitation of those lands to the "Dutch East India Company." Since several of the leaders of that powerful enterprise were in fact Jews, the Governor's ban was circumvented in a thousand different ways until it became a dead letter. Stuyvesant had to accept the fait accompli of the presence of this new community, which engaged in trade with the Indians—to whom it even sold weapons, despite the strict existing ban—but which, above all, was

---

138 R.E. Search: "*Lincoln Money Martired,*" p. 38.

139 Henry Ford: "*The International Jew.*"

occupied with lending money to the Dutch colonists. Nevertheless, eager to exercise maximum control over the activities of the newcomers, the Governor forced them to live apart from the colonists and the Indians, confining their residences to the island of Manhattan. Furthermore, to ensure that the separation was effective, Stuyvesant had a wall built in front of the Jews' houses; the street thus formed was called "Wall Street," and it is still known by that name today.

When New Amsterdam became New York—that is, when the Dutch had to leave the territory to the English—the Jews, though still marginalized, saw their situation improve. During the War of Independence, since the English accused the Jews of supporting the American rebels, the Jews fled en masse to Philadelphia, but as soon as the war ended, almost all of them returned to New York, sensing with their remarkable intuition that this city was destined to become the commercial and financial center of the world. Today, New York is the world's leading Jewish city.

During the Civil War, the Jews unanimously sided with the Northern states, but their political choice did not make them forget their business acumen; so, for example, when Lincoln and his Secretary of the Treasury went to visit the moneylenders, based in their increasingly flourishing "Wall Street," requesting their financial assistance to wage war against the secessionist Southern states, they received the following response: "War is a problematic and risky business, but we can lend you money, secured by land or crops, at 36 percent interest"[140]. And no matter how much Lincoln criticized their conduct, he had to hear this cynical reply: "If the Government does not want to buy the money at that price, we can sell it to the Confederate States of America"[141]. Lincoln refused to bow to the demands of the money barons and met with a friend of his, a Chicago lawyer, Colonel Dick Taylor, who was considered an expert on economic matters. Taylor told Lincoln that his problem was a false problem, and that he needn ly worry if the financiers did not want to lend him money. All Lincoln had to do was get Congress to pass a law authorizing the issuance of United States banknotes, which would have the same legal tender status as the

[140] Appleton's Encyclopedia, 1861, p. 296. Quoted by Alexander Del Mar in *"Science of Money."*

[141] R. E. Search: Ibid. Id. Op. Cit., p. 44.

currency issued by the bankers of the private institution called the "Bank of the United States." It seems that Lincoln asked his friend hesitantly, "Do you think people will accept those notes?" to which Taylor replied, "They will have no choice, if you make them legal tender. They will enjoy the legal sanction of the Government and will be as good and as acceptable as any other currency."[142]. Thus came into circulation the so-called "greenbacks," Lincoln's green banknotes, which, being born free of the burden of debt inherent in bank money, were to provide America with an era of great prosperity, despite the Civil War.

142 Correspondence between Abraham Lincoln and Colonel Taylor, 1891. Quoted by Wycliffe B. Vennard, in "*Conquest or Consent.*"

THE ASSASSINATION OF LINCOLN

Even though some European financiers supported the Confederate South, including the Rothschilds of Paris and London, others, such as the Lazards and the Hambros, financed the sale of arms from certain European states to the "Unionists" of the North. But what is beyond any doubt is that International Finance, as such, desired the victory of the Northerners. The attitude of the Wall Street magnates toward Lincoln—demanding a 36 percent interest rate—or the support of two branches of the Rothschilds for the Southerners did not conflict with—could not conflict with, even if they had wished it—the designs of High Finance, for if the Rothschilds helped the South directly, they helped the North indirectly just as much, if not more. But, in fact, what High Finance could not allow was the political dominance, or independence, of the Southern states, whose economy was based on agriculture—cotton, sugarcane, grains—and could do without the debt-money of the financiers to survive. Politically, moreover, the Southern ideology was at odds with the System's nebulous liberalism. The aid provided by some financiers to the South—aid that was, in any case, limited, conditional, and usurious—was nothing more than a wise and prudent measure adopted by the System to cover itself in the event of a Southern victory. Playing with two decks is a ruse frequently used by the System's card sharps.

But while the financial establishment supported Lincoln on the one hand, it attacked him on the other. It aided him with massive shipments of war supplies, yet insidiously undermined him by organizing political smear campaigns against him. These campaigns reached their peak when Lincoln decided to shut down the so-called "Bank of the United States."

The London newspaper "The Times," then the mouthpiece of the Financial Establishment, published the following editorial under the headline "Lincoln's Greenbacks": "If this pernicious financial policy, consisting of the creation of money by the State, which is being carried out in the American Republic, remains in effect, it will eventually be able to issue its own money at no cost. It will have all the money necessary to conduct its commerce. It will pay all its debts and never incur them again. America will become the most prosperous country in the world; moreover, its prosperity will be unparalleled by anything seen to date. "This government (of Lincoln) must be destroyed, or it will destroy us"[143]. As can be seen, the policy of the System's holders could not be stated more bluntly. Such cynicism should come as no surprise, since the "Gods" of Finance are well aware that the ignorance of the general public—and even of much of the elite—regarding financial matters is invincibly profound.

Ten days after Congress passed the law authorizing the circulation of "greenbacks," eighteen bankers from New York, Boston, and Philadelphia met in Washington, and after two days of study and consultation, drafted a circular that was sent to all members of the American "banking fraternity." This document, known as the "Hazard Circular"—named after one of the signatories—stated, among other things:

"Slavery will likely be abolished after this war; we refer to personal slavery. Both we and our European friends are in favor of this, since slavery represents the ownership of labor, but it also entails caring for the workers, whereas the plan of our European colleagues, led by England, is for Capital to control labor through the control of wages."

"The massive debt that we capitalists are securing as a result of this Civil War must be used to control the value of money. To achieve this, government bonds must be employed as the basis, or backing, of money. We cannot, for the moment, prevent the free circulation of 'greenbacks,' but we can control government bonds and, through them, the issuance of banknotes"[144].

This sensational document—but especially the transcribed paragraphs—should be carved in stone at the entrance to every bank in the world. It deserves to be read ten times in a row, because every sentence, every word, is brimming with profound meaning. Let us marvel, for example, at the humanitarian spirit of the bankers, who rejoice in the abolition of slavery, not because it is immoral, but because slave owners, under the law in force, also provide for them and their

---

[143] Quoted by C.K. Howe in *"Who Rules America?"* p. 77.

[144] Document cited by R.E. Search in *"Lincoln Money Martyr,"* pp. 47–48, and by Ferdinand Lundberg in "America's Sixty Families," p. 60.

families for life[145] while under the new system, advocated by "our colleagues in Europe" (the Rothschilds), Capital will control "labor" through the control of wages. Let us observe how the signatories of the Hazard Circular acknowledge that they themselves are ensuring that the Civil War among Americans results in a massive Public Debt, and that such Debt will be used to control the value of Money. To achieve this, since "for the time being" they cannot prevent the free circulation of government money (greenbacks), they will use bonds as the basis of money, and through this, they will thus control the issuance of banknotes.

Money would soon circulate among the "Founding Fathers," to the point that a venal Congress, two months after the meeting of the eighteen bankers who authored the Hazard Circular, passed an "Exception Clause Act" (Exception Clause Act) which stipulated that the next issuance of "greenbacks" was authorized and, as always, such banknotes would be "good for paying all kinds of debts, both public and private, except for customs duties on imports and interest on government debts." As can easily be understood, this clause forced the government to accept that its own money would be refused when customs duties were due, precisely at a time when, because of the war, arms and supplies had to be constantly imported from Europe. Furthermore, the clause gave bankers the long-sought excuse to reject the government's money, claiming that their clients would not accept it because it was not "hard currency." Thus Lincoln was forced to pass through the banks' Caudine Forks, stating that he could not "fight two wars at the same time, against the Confederates on the front lines and against the bankers in the rear, especially since it was clear that, of the two, the Confederates were, by far, the more honorable"[146]. And, paying

[145] It was not only the law that compelled slave owners to care for their slaves and their families, but common sense as well. In those days, slave traders had to purchase slaves from tribal chiefs in the Gulf of Guinea; they had to charter a ship and make the Atlantic crossing while evading pirates and privateers. Moreover, a human cargo was decimated, on average, by twenty percent during the voyage, due to disease and the conditions of the journey. In short, a slave necessarily cost a great deal of money, especially if sold on the condition that his family be purchased as well. And no one mistreats what has cost them dearly, unless, of course, they are mentally unstable or a sadist. With emancipation, however, slaves became workers of the capitalist system—that is, free citizens who can be thrown out onto the street whenever it suits the company. We do not defend slavery, but we do defend the Truth.

[146] R.E. Search: Op. cit. Ibid. Id. p. 49.

36 percent interest, he then obtained all the "money" he wanted. Simultaneously, the Financial System's loans to the Confederate States began to shrink[147].

R.E. Search, Lundberg, Del Mar, repeatedly cited, and Vincent C. Vickers[148], reproduce "in full" a letter written by the London banking firm "Rothschild Brothers" to the Wall Street bankers Moses Ikleshiemer, Randolph Morton, and Jacob Vandergould, giving them the necessary instructions for the creation of a new "Central Bank" that would not only replace but also improve upon the one created under the auspices of Alexander Hamilton and abolished by Abraham Lincoln. The letter recommends not repeating the previous "mistake"; that is, it is not enough for the "Central Bank" to be recognized by the Government, but it is also necessary for the Government to legalize it, to establish it by an act of Congress. It also recommends the elimination of "greenbacks," the currency issued by the Government. And, indeed, a Congress—half ignorant of financial matters, half "bribed" with the System's money—voted shortly thereafter on a "Contraction Act," authorizing the Secretary of the Treasury to issue 5 percent bonds, thereby enabling the withdrawal, over twenty years, of all currency from the United States, which was to be burned. In this way, the country's national currency would be destroyed and replaced by debt-money, in accordance with the System's designs. But it was not enough for the System to have neutralized the work of its opponent, Lincoln; it had to make an example of him.

On April 14, 1865, while attending a play in Washington, President Lincoln was shot and killed by a man named John Wilkes Booth. Shortly thereafter, Booth's lifeless body was found in a hayloft. Naturally, the crime was blamed on the Confederates, who had been defeated in the Civil War, since after emptying his revolver's magazine into Lincoln's body, Booth shouted, "Long live the South!" However, the truth was that Lincoln was in favor of treating the defeated with courtesy, and his death was, for the Confederates, a disaster nearly as great as their military defeat. It is also true that Booth never fought in the Confederate armies; he lived primarily in Canada, where he was approached by a certain Rothberg, an agent of the Rothschilds in

---

[147] Alexander Del Mar: Op. cit. Ibid. Id., p. 86.

[148] Vincent C. Vickers: *"Economic Tribulation,"* p. 142.

Ottawa, who gave him money and facilitated his move to the United States. Booth was an unstable and unbalanced character, a second-rate actor burdened with debt. Suddenly, he is seen living in opulence, assassinates the President, goes to the hideout where he has been assured impunity and a return to Canada, and there he is executed and his lips are sealed forever. Rothberg, the mastermind of the plan, returns to Ottawa: mission accomplished. Who was Booth? It is known that his family was Methodist, although the Baptists buried him in a cemetery reserved for Freemasons. But "among his ancestors were Jews. The rabbis of Washington were convinced that he was a Jew, noting that he used to join them in religious services at the synagogue, speaking Hebrew fluently"[149].

[149] Lloyd Lewis: "*Myths of Lincoln,*" p. 62.

THE "FEDERAL RESERVE"

On November 22, 1910, a group of financiers met on Jay Island, in the state of New Jersey. Among them were Senator Nelson Aldrich, of the rubber and tobacco trust; Abraham Piatt Andrew, economist and assistant to the U.S. Secretary of the Treasury; Frank Vanderlip, President of the National City Bank of New York; Henry P. Davison, a prominent employee of the "John Pierpont Morgan" banking firm; Charles D. Norton, President of the "First National City Bank," part of the Morgan trust; Benjamin Strong, Morgan's deputy; and Paul Moritz Warburg, a partner in the increasingly powerful New York banking firm "Kuhn, Loeb and Co." These powerful gentlemen drafted the plan for a "Federal Reserve Bank," whose official facade would conceal, in the public eye, its true nature[150].

On December 21, 1913, while most members of Congress were spending the Christmas holidays at home, the so-called "Federal Reserve Act" was passed in a manner that was nothing short of surreptitious; this act was nothing other than the draft drawn up by the nine individuals mentioned above. Broadly speaking, this law authorized the establishment of the Federal Reserve Corporation, a private entity with private initial funding, and governed by a Board of Directors known as the "Federal Reserve Board." This law stripped Congress of the right to create and control money, granting that power to the "Federal Reserve Corporation." The pretext given for the passage of this unusual law was "separating monetary policy," but the reality was that, in a great "democracy" often presented as the ideal prototype of that form of government, the power to create and control money was taken away from the "representatives" of the people and granted to a private corporation. And we do not believe it is a rash judgment to think that a private corporation will, by definition, tend to seek its own profit, whether or not this coincides with the general interest of the nation[151]. From a legal standpoint, moreover, the agreement reached was illegal,

---

[150] Eustace Mullins: *"A Study of the Federal Reserve,"* Omnia Veritas Ltd, www.omnia-veritas.com

[151] J. Bochaca: *"Finance and Power,"* Omnia Veritas Ltd.

since, when it was voted on in Congress, there was no necessary "quorum," and the majority of the representatives present had been bribed[152].

But how does the "Federal Reserve Board" operate? What is its "modus operandi"? The Federal Government, having spent more money than it collects from its citizens through taxes, needs, let's say, one billion dollars. The Government turns to the "Federal Reserve" and requests the one billion. The "Federal Reserve" agrees to the loan with interest. Then Congress authorizes the Treasury Department to print one billion dollars in U.S. Treasury bonds, which are then handed over to the Federal Reserve bankers. Next, the Federal Reserve pays the costs of issuing the one billion—perhaps five hundred dollars in ink and paper—and makes the exchange. And the government uses the billion dollars to meet its obligations. What are the consequences of this fantastic transaction? Simply that the United States government has indebted the people to the Federal Reserve Board for one billion dollars, plus accrued interest, until it is paid off. Since transactions like this, or similar to this, have been taking place from 1913 to the present, we find that now, after 63 years, the "sovereign" people of the United States are in debt to "their" Federal Reserve for more than $400 trillion, which accrues interest amounting to nearly $2 trillion per month[153]. As we state elsewhere[154], one hundred ninety-five million Americans are irretrievably in debt to some eight thousand other Americans. And we say "irretrievably" because it is not possible to pay even the interest on the debt, and the total amount of the debt exceeds even the real value of all the country's wealth.

We have said that the beneficiaries of the Federal Reserve number about eight thousand people. Obviously, we include in that figure senior banking officials throughout the United States. Ultimately, however, the true "gods" of American finance—which works in concert with international finance—the "Establishment," as it is called in America, or the System, as it is known in Europe, are, at most, a couple of dozen people, whom we will name later.

---

152 Sheldon Emry: "*Billions for the Bankers: Debts for the People*".

153 Sheldon Emry: Op. Cit. and James C. Oliver: "*A Treatise on Money*".

154 J. Bochaca: Op. Cit., p. 17.

It follows from the above that the power—not merely financial, but political—of these men is immense. Since Money is Power, and even more so in an era as materialistic as the present one, the Federal Reserve Board can determine the policy to be followed, without the publicity spectacles known as elections having any significance whatsoever. Both presidential candidates have had to turn to the masters of Money to present themselves before "the People." And no one gives anything for nothing, least of all a financier. Who, moreover, demands guarantees. But in any case, and increasingly so, decisions in America—the model of democracies—are ultimately made by men who have never been elected by the People. Who, for example, elected Kissinger? Who elected Rockefeller? Who elected Bernard Mannes Baruch, the so-called "proconsul of Judea in America" and mentor to Wilson, Hoover, Roosevelt, Truman, and Eisenhower?[155].

[155] A very recent example is the so-called "Watergate Affair." Under the pretext that President Nixon had lied when he claimed he was unaware that his henchmen were spying on Democratic Party voters, a sensational smear campaign was unleashed that culminated in the President's forced resignation. The architects of the campaign were two journalists: one, a Jew, Bernstein. The other, an Anglo-Saxon, Woodward, though employed by the pro-Zionist *"New York Times,"* owned by a Russian Jew, Sulzberger, who goes by the name Harrison. What were the real motives behind Nixon's political execution? Was it for failing to support Israel as expected in the last war with Egypt? Because if he had to resign for being "caught" in a web of lies, all his predecessors—especially Roosevelt—should have been shot, and instead they were elected and reelected. But the "miracle" is that in this whole affair, the only one who has come out "clean" is Kissinger. Kissinger! The man who knows everything knew nothing about Watergate. Oh, the depths of democratic idiocy!

A CENTURY OF HIGH-STAKES FINANCIAL POLITICS

From 1917 to the present day, over the course of the last fifty years, the System's interference in international politics has been so brazen that it has taken a veritable miracle of collective hypnosis on a global scale to keep it hidden from the eyes of so-called public opinion. Not even a Gustave Le Bon, who did not exactly harbor many illusions about the common sense of the individual lost in the Mass, could have believed what we see today: of course, Le Bon could not have imagined the massive growth of the "mass media" (journalism, radio, film, television) and their rational use for political ends. For the fact is that so-called public opinion knows nothing of the preponderant—indeed, decisive—role played by the System over the last fifty years.

If, on the one hand, Finance's control over the Economy has grown to the point of completely prostituting it, its influence over High Politics has also been steadily increasing, to the point of true enslavement in the case of the United States of America, a country subjected to the most abject domination by the members of the System. Two absurd world wars, in whose provocation and outcome the System played such a significant role, have made the United States the most powerful country on the planet. But its power is used solely against the interests of Europe and for the benefit of State Capitalism—or Slavery—known as Communism, which was established in Russia by the System itself.

This is not the place to dwell on the motivations, real and hidden causes, and outcome of World War I. To lift the veil on that horrible tragedy, it suffices to quote the words spoken by Alfred Moritz—who later changed his name to Mond upon settling in England and received the title of Lord Melchett—before the Zionist Congress, meeting in New York on June 14, 1928:

> "If I had told you in 1913 that the Austrian Archduke would be assassinated and that, along with all that would follow from such a crime, there would arise the opportunity, the possibility, and the occasion to create a national home for us in Palestine... you would have taken me for an idle dreamer. But... Has it occurred to you to think how extraordinary it is that from all that confusion and all that blood our

opportunity was born? Do you really believe that all of this—which has brought us back to Israel—is merely a coincidence?.."[156].

The fact that the perpetrator of the crime, a nihilist named Gavrilo Princip, as well as four of the six accomplices involved in the assassination, were fellow believers of the noble Lord, Chairman of the colossal trust "Imperial Chemical Industries," is revealing, though not decisively conclusive. What was decisively probative was that the result of that stupid catastrophe that was World War I was the legal recognition of a "Jewish National Home" in Palestine, and the establishment of State Capitalism, or Communism, in Russia.

Much has been written about the participation of International Jewish Big Capital in the preparation, execution, and consolidation of the Soviet Revolution in Russia. It is not the subject of this study to repeat here testimonies in support of this thesis. Elsewhere[157] we cite thirty-five such testimonies, fifteen of them from Jews, and the other twenty from entities and figures whom not even the wildest imagination would dare to label as anti-capitalists or anti-Semites, according to whom the "Russian" Revolution was in reality the work of the System. We shall mention here only, "pour mémoire," a report from the American Secret Service, transmitted by the General Staff of the French Army[158], in which, apart from noting that among the thirty-four leading figures of the First Soviet established in the USSR, thirty-one were Jews, the names of the bankers who financed the Revolution in the future USSR are cited: Jacob Schiff, Max Breitung, Felix Warburg, Otto H. Kahn, Mortimer Schiff, Jerome H. Hanauer, and the banking firms Kuhn, Loeb and Co. of the Federal Reserve Board, the Rhenish-Westphalian Banking Union, Lazard Frères, Gunzbourg, Speyer, and Nya Banken, the Rothschilds' correspondent in Northern Europe. All these banking firms are Jewish-, and are mentioned as such in that official document.

---

[156] Nesta H. Webster: "*Secret Societies and Subversive Movements*." Quoted by J. Bochaca in "*The History of the Vanquished*," Omnia Veritas Ltd.

[157] J. Bochaca: "*The History of the Vanquished*," chap. II. Omnia Veritas Ltd.

[158] This document is archived under reference 7-618-6 np 912. S.R. II. Transmitted by the Army General Staff. Deuxième Bureau. It is also in the Library of Congress, and has been reproduced by "*The* Times" in London (February 9, 1918) and in New York (May 1, 1922, and December 31, 1923).

* * *

Following World War I came several years of feverish reconstruction, with its—in the capitalist system—inevitable corollary: credit inflation, which, in turn, would lead to monetary deflation. The result of all this was the "economic" crisis of 1929, which began on "Black Friday" on the New York Stock Exchange and would last, at a minimum, for five years, throughout the world.

In Germany, following the Kaiser's forced abdication, the so-called Weimar Republic was in power. It is impossible to imagine a regime more clinically democratic than that one; it is impossible for there to ever again exist—apart from today's democratic United States—a regime more abjectly submissive to the dictates of the System: the absolute dominance of high finance; rampant inflation; unemployment reaching a record six million workers out of work; a proliferation of political parties; artistic and social degeneration; a Jewish community representing less than 0.9% of the population, yet controlling the banking sector, key government and administrative posts, and alone accounting for more than a third of the national income. Under these circumstances, the young National Socialist German Workers' Party, led by Adolf Hitler, entered the elections with a clear program: the elimination of the consequences of the infamous Versailles Diktat; the suppression of Marxist parties; the fight against degeneration in all its forms; the exaltation of the Race; the affirmation of the principle of nationalities and the consequent formation of Greater Germany; and the elimination of worker unemployment, for which he considered it essential to abandon the capitalist system and its tool, the gold standard, replacing it with the labor standard. Hitler's economic theories represented a return to the Natural Order of the Economy and, at the same time, the crushing of the System in Germany. The Führer presented, in his program, the theories of the economist Gottfried Feder, whose major works *Kampf gegen die Hochfinanz* and *Der Deutsche Staat auf nationaler und socialer Grundlage* have been practically banned from public libraries in this era of democratic freedom.

Following his very democratic electoral victory, however, Hitler applied his economic principles with great caution. His political instinct, rooted in "," told him that a radical application of Feder's principles would provoke a brutal reaction from the System and the governments of the countries subservient to it. Consequently, he removed Feder from leadership positions and instead called upon

Schacht—the perfect embodiment of the "dapper" capitalist, monocle and all—and decided to proceed in stages.

To begin with, the banking sector's power to grant or restrict credit at will was curtailed, and very low limits were placed on interest rates. The Reichsbank's issuance of currency was based on production, not on gold reserves, which did not exist. Classical Economics, under such circumstances, would have required a gold loan from any foreign bank or government; Hitler did not proceed in this manner, which provoked the amused curiosity of "economists" in Germany and abroad. "Germany's gold is the working capacity of its people," was a phrase of Hitler's, deemed demagogic by economists, though it caused natural apprehension in the circles of the System, which thrive on such a belief.

The corporatization of German agriculture was declared an urgent measure, because it was considered that national reconstruction required, as an indispensable condition, the existence of a strong class of farmers[159]. Within a few months, the mass of six million unemployed was absorbed, and labor even had to be imported from democratic France and Belgium. In six years of National Socialism, Germany moved from the back of the pack to the forefront of the world's industrialized nations... all without gold, without colonies... and without the cheap labor provided by the latter.

Meanwhile, in Italy, Benito Mussolini's fascist regime, even though it had begun its governmental activities ten years earlier, in 1923, did not achieve such astonishing successes in the economic sphere, although it did achieve them to a notable degree. Fascism placed greater emphasis than National Socialism on corporatist doctrines—as did Dr. Salazar in Portugal—but it did not challenge the gold standard. Fascist leaders recognized that the gold standard was irrational and outdated and wished to replace it with the silver standard, relying on the greater abundance of that metal and the fact that it was, therefore, more difficult for a few to hoard. It was sufficient, however, for Fascism to exercise strict control over the banks' credit policies, nationalize the Bank of Italy, ban Marxist parties, dissolve secret societies—sending the Grand Master of Italian Freemasonry into exile on the Lipari Islands—and severely punish all kinds of crimes, including economic ones, so that Italy might experience a period of prosperity unprecedented until then...

---

[159] Vicente Gay: "*The National-Socialist Revolution*," p. 269.

and since then.

But the danger was not Italy, but Germany; and not only because of the latter's greater stature and influence in every respect, but also because of its economic and financial doctrines, which, if they proved dangerous, were likely to prove fatal… once they could be implemented with the desired rigor. For this reason, as soon as Hitler came to power, the System unleashed a full-scale economic and diplomatic war against Germany. Its example could not be allowed to spread among its neighbors. In Belgium, Norway, Hungary, Romania, Yugoslavia, and Bulgaria, movements were emerging that declared themselves anti-capitalist, anti-communist, and anti-Semitic and proclaimed their desire to free their homelands from the deleterious influence of the System. This was the cause—the sole cause—of World War II. Germany had to be brought down urgently because the consolidation of the Hitler regime represented the destruction, forever, of the Gold Standard, the System's great tool of domination[160].

A curious parallel can be drawn between Napoleon and Hitler. Both clashed with the System, although the Great Corsican was fortunate that, in his time, it had not yet become as formidable a force as it would become in our century. Both, too, sought above all else—and despite everything—an alliance with England, but were defeated diplomatically by the System, which managed to enlist mighty Albion in its service. If Napoleon proposed to England, in the Peace of Amiens, to limit his naval power to one-third of Britain's, Hitler, in the Anglo-German Naval Treaty, did exactly the same. Hitler, like Napoleon, made such a gesture without any British concession in return, as a sign of goodwill and his peaceful intentions. And if Napoleon was able to secure the long-awaited peace with England simply by agreeing to return to the gold standard and allow the Bank of France to operate freely as a private entity, Hitler was offered, in the midst of war, a cessation of hostilities based on a stalemate peace, with only two conditions. What were those conditions? The British government demanded that the Reich renounce its economic autarky and adopt the gold standard, returning to the free-trade system. Furthermore,

[160] To some, this may seem an immature assertion, too at odds with what we have been told were the causes of World War II; however, as I cannot address this aspect in detail here, I refer the reader to my book *"The History of the Vanquished,"* where they will find the relevant documentation to form their own judgment on the matter.

Germany was to authorize the reopening of the Masonic lodges, which had been closed by Hitler. In return, the Allies would recognize the reannexation of Danzig to the Reich. Hitler's refusal to accept those conditions thwarted the peace[161].

We do not wish to dwell on the achievements, the fantastic accomplishments of National Socialism. Others have already done so in numerous works; the author as well, in the aforementioned book *The History of the Vanquished*. Suffice it to say here that Hitler's National Socialism was, to date, the last attempt to free a country from the chains of Gold. And that war was declared against it for opposing the System ideologically and practically, and for seeking territorial expansion at the expense of Communist Slavery, or State Capitalism, a creature of the former.

Following the "Victory" of the Democracies—in reality, a victory for the System and a general defeat—the mechanisms aimed at creating a World Super-Government, the United Nations and its many agencies, would be set in motion. As we mentioned in the section "The Breeding Ground," globalism is one of the components of the system, whose ultimate goal is not Industry, nor Commerce, nor Finance, nor making money... nor Capitalism, nor Communism, nor Zionism, but simply the Rule of the World over a human flock that has been dumbed down, massified, and democratized...

---

[161] Colonel J. Creagh-Scott of the Intelligence Service, who personally took part in the peace negotiations with German plenipotentiaries, mentioned these events in the highly authoritative bulletin of the "National Industrial Development Association of Eire," and later in a lecture delivered at Chelsea Town Hall. The French magazine "*Défense de* l'Occident," May 1953, p. 31, recalls these events and states that it was under explicit pressure from the Jewish banker Sir Montagu Norman, former Governor of the Bank of England, that Churchill proposed to Roosevelt the mandatory adoption of the gold standard, incorporating it into the Atlantic Charter.

WHO ARE THEY...?

"And the Lord said: I will cause the Gentiles to submit to My People, and they will bring their sons in their arms and their daughters on their shoulders. The Kings, O Israel! will be your foster fathers, and the queens will be the mothers who nurse you: all will prostrate themselves before you with their faces to the ground, and lick the dust from your feet..."

"...and the nation and the kingdom that do not submit to you shall perish; indeed, those nations shall be utterly destroyed... and you, Israel, shall suck the milk of the Gentiles and the breasts of kings..."

(Isaiah, XLIX, 22, 23 – LX, 10, 12, 16)

So far we have spoken of the System, or the "Establishment," of some of its ways of operating and its aims. We will now provide a list of the individuals and entities that comprise it.

Above the men with real power—who manipulate the Presidents and outlive them politically, such as U.S. Secretary of State Kissinger, and the President of the State Bank of the Soviet Union, Viktor Aschberg, as well as other lesser figures, there operates a sort of World Super-Government, parallel to the Official World Government—the nefarious United Nations—and which, due to the location of its founding, Bilderberg, in the Netherlands, is known as the "Bilderberg Group."

This association of extremely powerful men exerts, in a barely veiled manner, influence over governments throughout the world. Its purpose is to support the UN in the creation of a World Superstate. This Super-State, moreover, will be super-capitalist—that is, communist—since there is no initiative by the "Bilderbergers" that does not aim, directly or indirectly, to benefit the so-called Communist Bloc.

Here are the names of the most prominent members of this extremely powerful Bilderberg Group:

-Prince Bernhard of the Netherlands.

-Eugene Black, President of the International Bank[162].

-Robert McNamara, current President of the International Bank and former employee of the Rockefeller clan.

-Paul G. Hoffman, U.S. Ambassador to the UN. Senior executive at Goldman, Sachs and Co.; former administrator of the Marshall Plan and President of "Studebaker."

-Per Jacobson, President of the International Monetary Fund[163].

-Henry Kissinger, U.S. Secretary of State. Former employee of the Rockefeller family since the age of 23.

-Imbriani Longo, Governor of the Bank of Italy.

-Gabriel Hauge, economic "advisor" to Presidents Eisenhower, Kennedy, Nixon, and Ford.

-Michael Heilperin, economic and financial "advisor" to President Johnson. Senior executive at the banking firm Dillon and Co., owned by the Dillon (Lapowski) financial family.

-Walter J. Levy. Of Rockefeller's "Standard Oil of New Jersey."

-Sydney Weinberg. Banker. Member of the "inner circle" of the System's highest echelons of power.

-Lewis L. Strauss, Chairman of the U.S. Atomic Energy Commission. Member of the "Council on Foreign Relations," affiliated with the Rockefeller family.

---

[162] The International Bank is a kind of Central Bank of central banks, on a global scale.

[163] The International Monetary Fund finances newly decolonized countries and communist regimes.

-Chas. E. Salzman, director of the bank "Kuhn, Loeb and Co."

-Eric M. Warburg. Banker.

-Alexander Sachs. Banker.

-Gerard Swope. Banker.

-Isadore Lupin, economist, member of Nixon's Privy Council.

-Herbert Bayard Swope, banker.

-David Rockefeller, banker.

-Nelson Aldrich Rockefeller, banker.

-Dean Rusk, former U.S. Secretary of State.

-Paul Van Zeeland, former Prime Minister of Belgium. Former employee of "Banque Lambert," Rothschild's trustee in Brussels.

-Thomas S. Lamont, banker.

-William S. Paley (Palinski) and

-David Sarnoff, the two leading figures in American television.

-Arthur Harrison Hays (Sulzberger), editor of the "New York Times"

-General Lyman L. Lemnitzer, of the United States Joint Chiefs of Staff.

-Harry Guggenheim, banker.

-Harold K. Ginsberg, an employee of the Rockefeller family's "C.F.R."

-Hermann Baruch, brother of the former "mentor to presidents," Bernard Mannes Baruch. Banker.

-Henry Morgenthay, Jr., of the "Modern Industrial Bank."

Obviously, this list is incomplete. But the main figures are on it. We have referred, above, to an inner circle of the System. In fact, the financial world operates in a Masonic style. It proceeds by degrees. Ultimately, there is undoubtedly an "innermost circle" about which perhaps no one knows anything—or perhaps they do—because the perfection of the System's "modus operandi" has made secrecy practically unnecessary. In any case, here are the members of what we know to be the innermost circle.

-The Federal Reserve Board, composed of the five currency-issuing banks of the United States. This group is controlled by the Warburg, Kuhn, Loeb, and Kahn families.

-Lehman Brothers. The largest banking institution in the world, second only to Kuhn, Loeb and Co. of the Federal Reserve.

-The Rockefeller Empire, which includes the "Standard Oil of New Jersey" oil trust, "Chase National Bank," and the Chilean copper mines "Anaconda Copper Co." It is a dominant force in the National City Bank and is connected, thanks to a shrewd policy of marriage alliances, to the Dodges (automobiles), the Stillmans (steel), the Aldriches (high finance), etc.[164]

-The Rothschild Empire, based in London, Paris, Vienna, and Frankfurt. Masters of the Rockefellers in their policy of marriage alliances. Nya Banken, in Stockholm, is considered their agent in Northern Europe. The Aschbergs, agents of Rothschild, have served as presidents, from father to son, of the Soviet State Bank since its founding in 1917. The family controls nickel production in New Caledonia. It also owns the mercury mines in Almadén (Spain).

-Lazard Bank, currently on par with Rothschild in importance. Highly influential in the European Economic Community and the

---

[164] The heavily Jewish-influenced Rockefeller family, with 50,000 bank branches worldwide—all direct or indirect descendants of the "Chase National Bank"—is said to earn two million dollars a minute. (According to Dr. Oren Fenton Potito in "*National Christian News*," No. 7, 1975.

former British Empire.

-The "United Fruit" empire of Samuel Zemurray, all-powerful in Central America and the Caribbean.

-The Melchett family, which controls the British chemical trust I.C.I., as well as nickel production in Canada.

-Goldman, Sachs and Co. The strongest of the American banks, following "Kuhn, Loeb" and "Lehman."

-The Oppenheimer trust, a South African financial firm. It owns gold mines and controls South African diamond production. It owns the "Hispanic" Rio Tinto mines.

-The Guggenheim trust, bankers, which controls, along with the Speyers, Bolivia's zinc, and, along with the Morgans, Chile's copper and potassium nitrate.

-The Speyers, bankers. Together with the Rockefellers, they control Mexico's oil.

-The Seligman family, who, together with the Goldschmidts, exploit the copper mines of Peru.

-The "Ford Motor Company" consortium, the leader of the global automotive industry. The heirs—children and grandchildren—of the founder of this industrial empire have joined forces, through family ties and shared interests, with other "clans" of the System. (If only the old "anti-Semite" Henry Ford could see this today!)

-The "Dillon-Read" Bank, whose president is Douglas Dillon (Samuel Lapowski).

-Stanley H. Ruttenberg, the labor "guru" of the AFL-CIO, the most powerful American labor unions.

-Charles B. Shuman, President of the American Farm Bureau Federation, the true dictator of American agriculture.

-Donald K. David, President of the "Committee for Economic

Development," an all-powerful, tax-exempt foundation sponsored by "Ford Motor Co."

-Hambros Bank of London, the largest "British" banking firm after N.M. Rothschild and Lazard Bros. On our continent, it is associated with the "French" Schneider banking group, which in turn controls the Le Creusot trust, involved in armaments and steel.

-S. Japhet and Co. Bank, founded in Germany in 1880 and relocated to London in 1896, which holds vast interests in the Arab world. Through the marriage of a daughter of Samuel Japhet to Lord Mountbatten of Burma, this family is related to the British Royal Family.

-Israel Moses Sieff, of "Political and Economic Planning"—a breeding ground for socialists—and of the colossal "Marks and Spencer" department stores.

-Sydney Bernstein, head of British Television (I.T.A.).

-Salomon Zuckerman, a "South African" billionaire and private advisor to Prime Ministers Wilson and Callaghan.

-The Vanderbilt-Whitney clan, American bankers, dominant in the global copper and steel sectors.

-The Gunzbourg Bank, Japan's leading banking institution.

-The Dreyfus family, "French." They are called "the kings of wheat."

- Paul Getty, England's wealthiest man.

-The "Vickers and Maxim" trust, created by an adventurer from Odessa, Sir Basil Zaharoff, the world's largest arms trust.

-The Morgan banking house, which ranks fifth among American banks and ninth worldwide.

-The Anglo-Dutch "Unilever" trust, founded by the Lever brothers and Simon Van den Bergh, which ranks first in the global market for margarine, oil, and soap.

-The Dutch Philips trust, the leading European electronics company, closely linked to the Rotterdamsche Bank and the "Unilever" trust, as well as to the "Royal Dutch" oil trust—founded by Henry Detterding and —and to Marcus Samuel's "Hell Petroleum."

-The Lambert family, Belgian Jewish bankers, closely linked to the Rothschilds.

With the exception of the Morgans, the Rockefellers, and the Fords, the other superpowers named are exclusively Jewish. As for Rockefeller, it is partially Jewish due to the marital and financial alliance of the father of the current Nelson Rockefeller with a daughter of the Jewish bankers Aldrich.

The above list of what we might call the World Super Government should probably be supplemented with the names of Sidney Weinberg and Eugene Blanck, financiers already mentioned, and the unknown leaders of the "Anti-Defamation League," a sort of Jewish Masonic organization with tremendous hidden power.

These dynasties of Money, as we have already said, are also interconnected by family ties or shared interests—and often both at the same time. In short, they represent some three hundred people at most, who select their successors through co-optation from among their own circle.

These are the "Gods" of the System. Their existence was already revealed by Rathenau, himself a member of the system, with his famous phrase: "Three hundred men, who know one another, govern the destinies of the European continent and choose their successors from among those around them." (Wiener Freie Presse, December 24, 1912). The fact that, in overwhelming proportion, the members of this sort of World Government belong to a specific ethnic group does not, of course, imply an indiscriminate accusation against all members of that group. But there is also no doubt whatsoever that if many, or a majority of them, are aware of the activities of that minority of "Gods" and their henchmen within the System and do not denounce them or oppose them, they become accomplices to it.

What is the goal, the ultimate goal, of these Gods of the System? History and daily events confirm it. The establishment of Communism on a global scale. In the early days, they aided Marx, Engels, Boerne, Lafargue, and other prominent communist apostles. They financed the Soviet Revolution in Russia. They supported communist movements in other countries, and continue to support them. They made the Bolshevization of China possible by forcing America to withdraw aid from Chiang Kai-shek, while Mao Zedong received it from Russia in abundance[165]. They finance, whenever necessary, communist states when the unnatural Marxist system finds itself on the brink of economic bankruptcy. "Trotskyist" Yugoslavia survives only thanks to American subsidies. RUSSIA DOES NOT GO HUNGRY THANKS TO AMERICAN AID. The price of American wheat and other grains skyrocketed in mid-1973 because the Nixon administration allowed grain speculators to sell them at rock-bottom prices and on credit to the Soviet Union and Red China. The U.S. government paid the difference between the political prices and the actual prices. In other words, the long-suffering American taxpayer paid so that their potential enemies would not starve to death. This implausible transaction was "arranged" by Kissinger during his trips to Beijing and Moscow[166]. It was also Kissinger who facilitated the sale—practically a financial gift from taxpayers via the U.S. Administration—of fertilizers to the USSR[167].

The System's aid to the USSR begins, as we have seen, with the establishment of the Soviet state in Russia, and continues with the Rockefeller-Stalin Pact, which allowed the communists to exploit their oil wealth and even market it in the Free World. Another financier, Averell Harriman, who attained great political influence under Roosevelt, developed the railway network in Russia. The "German" financier Rathenau agreed with Stalin to provide technical assistance from the Reich to the USSR, without any compensation, for the launch

[165] Rockefeller's "Amerasia" Organization caused the American Administration to make a complete about-face with its false reports on the situation in China. Owen Lattimore, later accused of communist activities, and General Marshall, one of the organizers of the Pearl Harbor fiasco, were the top (visible) figures responsible for handing China over to Communism.

[166] The Jew Michel Fribourg, nicknamed "the Cereal Emperor" and the richest man in America, was the only "American" to benefit from that incredible "deal."

[167] In this "deal" as well, the major beneficiary turned out to be a Jew, Armand Hammer (according to "*The Thunderbolt*," August 1973).

of the Soviet chemical industry.

In short, the System has always supported Communism. If the Iron Curtain were truly impenetrable in both directions, and the Communist Bloc were left isolated, it would not last even a couple of years. Only the support and loans from the West keep it afloat. Capitalism is a criminal system, but by allowing—with ever- ly greater obstacles—the existence of free and productive enterprise, it falls short of its true aims, which are none other than the enslavement of humanity with the most terrible weapon: Money. That is why Communism is fatally necessary, as the by no means "proletarian" Karl Marx affirmed, with tremendous and irrefutable logic, from within the System.

The System, whose mission transcends Capitalism, seeks the unification of the World through the Mongolization of peoples, races, and nations[168]. That is why its architects are "anti-racists," though only when it comes to the White Race, the bearer of Civilization and Culture. They advocate for the interbreeding of whites and blacks, for example, but in the artificial State of Israel, they have implemented racial laws in their favor that are far more drastic than Hitler's "Rassenschutz Gessetz." For this is the ultimate objective... This is the solution to the Enigma of Capitalism, always making deals with its supposed adversaries... Ultimately, interpreting biblical prophecies, there is nothing more than the Chosen People, ruling over a human flock—mixed-race and Mongoloid—sheared and bleating in unison.

---

[168] In tribal New Africa alone, with its sorcerers titled Presidents of the Republic, there are, today, 350 large American multinational companies and some 200 European ones. It seems strange that Big Capital would want to invest in laughable African "countries." Yet it does. Why? Because it cannot lose. In New York, there is the O.P.I.C. (Overseas Private Investment Corporation), which insures capitalist investments against expropriation by the aforementioned sorcerers. This organization is, in turn, guaranteed by the U.S. government, at Kissinger's initiative. Thus, the American people guarantee the multinationals against expropriation by tribal chiefs while simultaneously financing the economic development of those tribes with Western technology ("*South African Observer*," August 1976).

THE SOLUTION

After setting forth, in the collection of sections grouped under the title "Misery in Abundance," the reasons that clarify the apparent paradox of the West's current economic situation—with its overflowing stockpiles that cannot be consumed due to a lack of money—and then explaining, as succinctly as possible, the actions and identities of the actors in this drama, we will now propose the solution. That is to say, after answering the questions "What is happening?", "Why is it happening?", "Who is doing it?", and "Why are they doing it?", we now consider it our duty to provide the solution to the problem posed by this global nightmare. Not just any solution. THE SOLUTION.

It is likely—we are about to assert—that the greatest difficulty in understanding Economics lies in its overwhelming simplicity. In an absurd era such as the present one, the terminal phase of the transition from Culture to Civilization, an era of the transmutation of all values, in which words are losing their former meaning, Economics could not escape the general rule of the Organism to which it belongs[169]. The West, afflicted by a tremendous Cultural Parasitism[170], suffers, in its brain, from the disease of Liberalism, and from there radiate all the other evils afflicting the other organs: Democracy, in the Nervous System; Atheism, more or less disguised, in the Cardiovascular System; and Capitalism, in the Digestive System. If the Brain, the Nerves, and the Heart—though severely affected—still resist, the Stomach, the weakest part and the one that receives—due to the Enemy's interest and its intuition that this is the type of attack that best suits its idiosyncrasy—the most vicious assaults of the Great Parasite, is on the verge of collapse. A collapse that would cause the death of the

---

[169] A telling example of current economic policy is the fact that no one seems to have been surprised by the recent economic programs of the governments of two old European countries, England and Spain. On the one hand, they claim that we must fight unemployment, and on the other that we must save, and to make people save, they raise taxes. But fighting unemployment means increasing production. So we must increase production and decrease consumption. The authors of this program have not been committed to any mental institution.

[170] Francis Parker Yockey: "*Imperium,*" Omnia Veritas Ltd.

Organism.

We hate cowardly optimism at least as much as we hate irresponsible, pessimism, but we cannot escape the categorical moral imperative of our Realism, which compels us to proclaim, without mincing words, that if the measures of THE SOLUTION are not adopted soon—if they are not adopted now—the West will go down the drain before fulfilling its historical destiny, joining the Great Cultures that preceded it in the pantheon of History, once their life cycles have run their course.

The Solution, in reality, follows irrefutably from everything stated so far, that is, that if the ills of the Western Economy stem from:

a) from the private control of money
b) from the power of private entities to issue it.
c) from being based on a commodity of virtually zero intrinsic value, such as Gold, and
d) from the superstitious belief that the Machine must provide work for man

the Solution will consist in the simultaneous application of the principles contrary to the ills listed, namely:

a) public (state) control of money.
b) state issuance of money.
c) Basing Money on the Labor Standard, which we may also call the Wealth Standard.
d) Acceptance of the principle that the Machine must take work away from man, performing it in the best, fastest, and cheapest way possible.

* * *

We consider it useful to refer the reader to the section "Scope" at the beginning of this work and to remind them that we are referring to the West, and, more specifically, at least for the moment, to Europe, its core. We understand that politically, for now, we can only refer to "residual" Europe, west of the Iron Curtain, with its 320 million inhabitants, heirs to a millennia-old culture and bearers of civilization to every corner of the planet; r a partial Europe whose primary political objective must necessarily be the adoption of all measures aimed at the recovery of the dozen countries in the East of our continent, with their 150 million subjects dependent on Soviet state capitalism, established in Russia thanks to the aid provided by private capitalism based in the West. In other words, the Solution can only be implemented by a European State that relies on the structures of the current Common Market—which, with all its formidable flaws, at least has the merit of existing—and that gradually expands its sphere of action, fully implementing the positive political principles of the Treaty of Rome[171] until it turns into reality the dream of men so distant and disparate, in space and time, so different from one another and of such diverse value and standing, as Charlemagne, the Hohenstaufens of the Holy Roman Empire, Charles of Spain and Germany, Louis XIV, Napoleon, Hitler, and Adenauer: the European Nation.

One might object—as the eternally short-sighted are wont to do—that this is a utopia (and everything is, in truth, a utopia until it is put into practice), that the European Nation is not yet visible on the political horizon, and that the measures—whether political, on a general level, as well as economic ones at the level of a Community's digestive system—that are of interest now must pertain to the old mini-nations still existing, still vegetating, in Western Europe, remnants of ancient dynastic unions or "diplomatic accidents," and in whose active existence those nostalgic for Grandfather's hyper-nationalism like to believe. To these determined believers in national atomism, we must simply and swiftly remind them of two things, namely:

a) that the sine qua non of a nation's existence is sovereignty, that is, independence; and this is not, politically speaking, the mere emanation of an act of will, but rather the consequence of collective will backed by force. It is not enough to want to be independent; one must be able to be so. And today, whether nineteenth-century minds like it or not, only a political community with a population of at least two hundred million inhabitants, equipped with advanced technology—whether homegrown or imported—can be independent, and thus can be a free nation. From, in fact, today, in the world, there are only three true

[171]...And naturally forgetting the negatives, such as the ridiculous demand that the Community must practice the System of Inorganic Democracy with Universal Suffrage and a plurality of "parties."

nations: the USSR, the USA, and China[172]. And Europe can be, must be, one of them. The rest—the so-called Third World, or also "underdeveloped countries" (when one wishes to be polite), "sub-capable" (when one does not wish to be), or "blackmailing beggars" (when one wishes to speak the plain truth)—are mere extras, possessing only centripetal power, which they exercise over their subjects, but without centrifugal power, since they depend, officially or not, on one of the three nations mentioned. Thus, any old European "nation" that harbored any notions of economic independence would be automatically crushed[173] by the power within whose sphere of influence it found itself.

b) that the alternative to the creation of the European Nation is the disappearance, in the very near future, of our residual continent as a political entity. And not only as a political entity but even as a racial entity. Europe is threatened with disappearance; Europeans are in danger of physical extinction. If the European Nation is not created, the disappearance of Europe—economically, politically, and physically—will ensue. This is inevitable. The problem is not whether this will happen, but when. And everything suggests it will be soon, barring unforeseeable political changes outside Europe, or a brutal awakening of the American people against the Parasite that undermines their existence. Or do the deluded liberal-democrats perhaps believe that Europeans are going to stop the two hundred million Russians by regimenting a billion undernourished people of color who are at our doorstep, with a barrier of household appliances and passenger cars? Do they really believe the UN will stop them? But the UN is them!... The American umbrella? Please! It was enough for the Kennedy administration to dislike certain aspects of the Common Market and for Nixon's "entourage" to object to certain economic measures by Pompidou and the fantastic economic might of West Germany for them to, aside from tremendous economic retaliatory measures—such as the

---

[172] Capitalism, a tool of Zionism, is not, despite all its omnipotence, a nation. It aspires to World Power, pitting peoples against one another, but to be a true nation, its Soul (Finance) must be complemented by a Body (a territory and a numerically significant population). Israel is not a nation, but a Zionist outpost at the crossroads of three continents, next to the Suez Canal and the oil pipelines.

[173] Under any "democratic" pretext, by fomenting an internal revolt, as the U.S. did two years ago in Greece, or by provoking, through its propaganda and financial pressure, an electoral defeat, as happened to De Gaulle in 1968. Or without pretexts, brutally, as Russia did with Hungary in 1956, or with Czechoslovakia in 1970.

"Kennedy Round" and the devaluation of the dollar— they threatened, with unparalleled cynicism, to withdraw the Yankee troops protecting Europe under NATO. What a curious form of protection this is! For those with childish mindsets who imagine that the U.S. is a solicitous and good-natured Santa Claus, always ready to organize Crusades in defense of Democracy and the Rule of Law, it will suffice to refer them not to a history textbook, but to the newspapers of our time. Turkey, an ally of the U.S. and a member of NATO, was deprived of the American military support it had counted on in 1962, in exchange for the withdrawal of Soviet "missiles" from Castro's Cuba; immediately, Turkey, disarmed before its colossal neighbor, was forced to make tremendous political concessions to the USSR. To regain the Turks' favor, the U.S. had to miserably betray its Greek "ally," siding with the Turkish minority (them! So democratic!) in the case of Cyprus. What the American alliance is all about is well known in South Vietnam, abandoned to Communism in exchange for the easing of Soviet pressure in the Middle East; it is also known in Lebanon, abandoned to Syria on the condition that the latter eliminate the Palestinians, who are a nuisance to Israel, the only unconditional ally that Zionism allows—indeed, imposes—on the guests of the White House. The American umbrella! Let's be serious!... The System that governs, through imposed straw men in Washington, is only interested in Europe as a card to play in the game it is waging with the lords of the Kremlin, aimed at the establishment of a World Superstate—that is, at the realization of its negative ideals. On the day it suits Washington; when it suits the System—which, aside from its political and economic interests, viscerally hates Europe—or when it is forced to pay a certain price in exchange, for example, for the neutralization of communist agitators in Central and South America, Castro included, the price in question will likely be Europe. The "umbrella" will be withdrawn—Oh, yes! Of course it will! With a hundred signed documents "guaranteeing" our freedom... Of course!—and the Pentagon "boys" will go home, heeding the request of some European socialist imbecile, some Brandt, Callaghan, or Mitterrand, whose head will be the first to roll when his Soviet friends arrive, as a grotesque epilogue to an unprecedented historical drama.

We apologize for this lengthy digression, which we consider essential, given the short-sightedness we observe regarding this issue of the European nation. Today, there are no economically self-sufficient countries on our continent. Only Hitler's Germany could have been so forty years ago, but conditions were not the same as they are today, and in any case—as we have seen in the section titled THE SYSTEM—an international campaign of unprecedented violence was unleashed against the Reich, with economic, psychological, and political measures that culminated in the last World War, a veritable suicide of Europe and the West[174]. Let us not be pessimistic and consider that, if Germany, practically alone, was on the verge of victory, today, flanked by all the peoples of Europe and taking great care not to repeat past mistakes—and especially German, English, French, and other forms of hyper-nationalism—victory should be achieved. Moreover, in the face of a United Europe, the bellicose ambitions of non-European powers would undoubtedly diminish in intensity. The Great Parasite, deprived of its favorite weapon—the only one it can use—that is, Capitalism, would be like a scorpion without venom. Europe, the European Nation, is possible. It must be, since it is necessary. Those who say otherwise need not read on, and I regret, for their sake, that they have come this far. Without the European Nation, without a politically united Europe, there is no viable economic solution. Only collective ruin. And here, too, it bears repeating that the problem is not whether such ruin will occur, but when. And this is not only because capitalist contradictions and those of their false opposite—Marxist hyper- -bureaucratism—make such ruin fatally inevitable, but because even if that were not the case, even

174 "The big bankers were alarmed by the successes of Hitler's financial policy in Germany, just as several generations earlier their families had been frightened by the successes of the natural economy of Lincoln and Napoleon. What would have been a laudable progress for Germany and other countries following its example was, in reality, the main cause of World War II. The struggle between rival monetary policies was inevitable" (Carnelius Carl Veith, *"Citadel of Chaos,"* p. 286). "Marriner Eccles of the Federal Reserve Board and Montague Norman, Governor of the Bank of England, reached an agreement in 1935 on the policy to be employed to crush, by any means necessary, including war if necessary, Hitler's financial experiments" ("*The* Word" of Glasgow, August 3, 1949. Quoted by Thomas Porter: *"The Green Magicians."* "The two main causes of World War II were: First. The success of the German barter system. Second. Hitler's determination not to accept foreign loans. His declaration that Germany's business affairs would be conducted in the same manner as those of an honest merchant caused real panic in financial circles" (Francis Neilson: *"The Churchill Legend,"* p. 296). Finally, in an interview with Roosevelt, eleven days after the outbreak of hostilities in Poland, Bernard Baruch, the so-called "Proconsul of Judea" in America, told Roosevelt: "We must keep our prices low, even if we lose money, for in this way we will win the customers of the non-belligerent nations. It will be the only way to destroy the German barter system" (*New York Times*, September 14, 1939). But already a year before the outbreak of the war, Baruch himself stated publicly, during a tribute to George C. Marshall, that "we are not going to let that fellow, Hitler, get away with it. His monetary policy is a danger to everyone." (Francis Neilson: *"The Tragedy of Europe,"* p. 302).

if our poor reactionary-conservatives—whether on the right or the left—managed to find a semblance of a solution to their economic problems, such a solution would, by necessity, require the endorsement, the authorization, of the System. And it costs the System very little to bring recalcitrant Europeans to heel when any of them decide to act. But they could not prevail against a United Europe, governed by an elite of true statesmen. The Enemy's main strength lies in our weakness, stemming from Liberalism, the schizophrenia of a Culture's brain. As long as the mini-nationalism of the Old Man and the liberalism of the "village idiot" prevail, the Enemy's task will be very easy.

* * *

Returning, then, to the subject of this study, we will analyze the measures advocated for the establishment of a National-European Economy, or, if you prefer, a National-Socialist or National-Revolutionary one; the names matter very little to us.

We will begin with state intervention regarding the control and issuance of Money. When speaking of state control, we wish to make it clear that we are not referring to the nationalization of the banking system but, simply, we repeat, to its control. Or, more specifically, to the control of Money. We believe it has already been made sufficiently clear that if Money is an instrument for measuring and exchanging the wealth produced by a community, it must be issued as that wealth is made available to the market. As we have already indicated elsewhere, advances in information technology allow the issuance of Money—that is, its quantity—to be calculated with absolute precision. It is elementary that the greater the wealth created by a community, the greater the amount of money needed to distribute that wealth. But to know the exact amount of money needed to perform its distributive function, it is necessary to know exactly the amount of national wealth—that is, what actually constitutes national income.

The first thing to do, then, is to establish the National Balance Sheet. In other words, to take stock of the real credit of the Nation-Europe. This may seem, at first glance, unfeasible due to its sheer magnitude. But this is not the case. In an era like ours, in which European mini-states exercise absurd, excessive control over every sub, and can at any moment know the number of illiterate people, deaf-mutes, albinos, ambidextrous individuals, homosexuals, pedestrians, presbyopes, or Jehovah's Witnesses living within their mini-borders, it cannot be a

Herculean task to carry out a national inventory, using the compilations made by existing institutions such as the Land Registry, the Property Registry, the State Treasury, the Chambers of Commerce, local and municipal appraisal agencies, and, of course, the accountants of all the country's companies. In a word: Let us compile, using existing institutions—the aim is not to create more bureaucracy, but to eliminate it as much as possible—the value of the assets of what we might call "Europe, Limited Partnership," with its arable land, its forests, its factories, its workshops, its buildings, its livestock, its mines, its ships, its raw materials; its public utilities, such as its aqueducts and oil pipelines; bridges and roads; railways, reservoirs, ports, and fortifications; its raw materials, its manufactured goods. Let us add to this the human capital at our disposal. Indeed, a country's population also has a monetary value, for it is overwhelmingly evident that a factory, however perfect it may be, has no value whatsoever if there are no men to operate it and other men to consume its products. A person—leaving aside, of course, their other human dimensions—is a source of real wealth for the country, as both a consumer and a producer. In the past, one could say that a person was worth, in purely mechanical terms, one-tenth of a horsepower. But today, thanks to insurance companies, we have arrived at a figure that reflects the capital value of a given population. Thus, it can be said that, according to studies and averages conducted by the most important insurance companies, the market value of a European citizen aged about 25 or 30, healthy, of average education, and possessing normal common sense, can be calculated at some five million pesetas. The magnitude of this figure, when considering the entire population of the European Nation, should not alarm us. We have no need, nor any obligation, to convert that figure into money if we do not wish to. It is simply a matter of accounting—but true accounting, for accounting must reflect facts and realities. Adding both figures—the human value and the material value—we will have an amount that measures, in any monetary unit we choose—the eurofranc or the euromark, for example—the assets of real credit, of Capital, of real wealth, or of Assets—whatever we wish to call it—of the corporate entity Europe, Limited Partnership ( ).

But the Asset is nothing more than a symbol; a figure, certainly impressive, but a figure, after all. How that figure, which represents the Capital of a firm, Europe S. in C., should be spent or used is a matter that does not depend on the governing bodies of the European Economy. The latter is limited to making the economic resources available to the Total Organism of which it is a part, ensuring the proper functioning of the Digestive System. And nothing more. But also nothing less.

Naturally, there are two options. We can "monetize"—that is, issue the corresponding currency—all the assets of our European homeland, or we can "monetize" just a portion of them. Whichever path is taken—and this will depend more on political than economic reasons—one thing is evident by definition: the nation will not be living "beyond its means," as the economists of our unfortunate era like to repeat, like parrots, with unparalleled stupidity. That is to say, as long as wealth greater than that represented by the total figure reflected in the National Balance Sheet's Assets is not monetized and distributed—indeed, as long as it is not spent—the Nation would not be living beyond its means; it would not be biting off more than it can chew. It would be impossible for this to happen because simple, honest arithmetic would prevent it. And when, with the invaluable help of information technology, it became clear that the nation's "reserves" or assets were beginning to decline, that would be the moment to take measures to restore balance, since the wealth that Europe can produce without the straitjacket of finance is so immense that it is incredible. Let us bear in mind that, despite the last two stupid inter-European fratricidal wars; the loss of immense colonial empires; the human and economic bloodletting that this has entailed; the political and economic dependence on the yoke of the System, and the constant sabotage of our technology, perpetrated by the trade union "mafia" of all stripes, economic progress in Europe has managed to reach remarkable heights. If we possess an industrial capacity—which can equally be applied to agriculture—nearly fifty times greater than that of the turn of the century (as expressed by the number of horsepower that machinery yields to the European man today), it is irrefutable that we should be living fifty times better. I do not know if many fully realize what "fifty times better" or "fifty times more" actually means. I fear that the hyperbole of popular language has caused most people to lose their sense of numbers. But these figures, cold and stark, show us that the European, the Westerner, as soon as he frees himself from the yoke of Capitalism[175], will immediately attain a degree of economic prosperity that the short-sighted servants of the System cannot even conceive. Recall once again what Germany accomplished between 1933 and 1939, implementing, for political reasons, only a quarter (or perhaps

[175] And, naturally, of its false opposite, Marxism, or State Capitalism.

less) of the economic measures that were in the minds of its rulers; keep in mind that that formidable leap forward occurred despite the System's near-universal hostility and boycott, with its vast resources, and consider that in the thirty-seven years that have passed from 1939 to the present, science and technology have made decisive progress. What could not be achieved today, not by Germany alone, but by a United Europe?

We do not wish to leave this topic of state control and issuance of money without first clarifying that, as is logical, we must dispense with "Fake Money" or Credit-Money invented by the Banking System. That is to say, when establishing the National Balance Sheet, existing Credit-Money must be taken into account, the total amount of which must be deducted from the Money to be issued by the State, in order to gradually eliminate it as bank "loans" are paid off. In this way, a sound—that is, STABLE—currency will be achieved in the short term, the duration of which no longer concerns the Economic Body, but rather the Whole, or the Political Body. Since it will not have to absorb the burden with which it was created—its birth defect, Debt, the primary and[176] cause of rising prices and, consequently, of the erosion of the value of all currencies—Money will truly become the instrument of measurement and, from there, the medium of exchange of an unchanging value. If anything, the only possibility for Money to change in value and depreciate—apart, of course, from an inconceivable national debacle, an apocalyptic earthquake, a great drought, etc.—will lie in a gradual decline in a people's productive capacity, and in such a case it is no longer the responsibility of the Economic Body to adopt the relevant measures, but rather that of the Whole, or the Political Body. In the National-Revolutionary system of the Future Europe, any alteration in the value of our currency—in the short, medium, or even long term—will be, by pure logic and arithmetical, as impossible as a change in the value of the meter—which will always be worth one hundred centimeters—or the kilogram—which will always be worth one thousand grams. If its value is altered at all, it will be in relation to non-European or non-Western powers, which, if they progress—as is to be expected—at a slower pace than ours, will see their respective

[176] Eventually, the price of a certain item may rise, just as it may fall, due to changes in taste or the emergence of new substitute products, but such fluctuations—which may even be healthy as they foster fair competition—will be minimal.

currencies depreciate relative to ours[177]. But, in any case, this will be their problem, not ours.

An immediate effect of the abolition of this monstrosity of the capitalist economy—Debt-Money—will be a radical reduction in taxes. Let us not forget that, in our current mad system, the State, acting as a private individual, must turn—just like any private individual—to the banking system to borrow money or obtain credit. To repay those lines of credit, plus interest, it has no choice but to invariably turn to its subjects. Furthermore, with the state's gradual encroachment into private spheres, its demands for credit become increasingly urgent. Marxism—affectionately dubbed "Socialism" by the System's lackeys—takes care of its increasingly enfeebled subjects from the womb to the grave, thereby achieving a dual objective: on the one hand, it stifles private initiative, eliminates incentives, and, ultimately, halts Progress, and on the other, it makes its subjects dependent, in every way and for everything, on the omnipotent State. Well then: he who gives everything can take everything away. This Marxism is taking root in the residual Europe; frankly, when socialists come to power through elections; surreptitiously, when so-called "conservative" governments must fulfill, from the seat of power, the demagogic electoral promises. Marx advocated for the gradual increase of taxes, both on profits and on inheritances, as a means to establish the Dictatorship of the Proletariat. That Marx's program is being carried out by all the governments of Western Europe is so evident that it is not worth discussing.

Gottfried Feder said that "the ultimate goal of our state is the establishment of a tax-free society"[178], citing as an example the Regional State of Bavaria—which was certainly not among the wealthiest in Germany—whose state treasury was built without a single pfenning of tax[179]. In other words, what Bavaria obtained from the exploitation of public forests and gardens, railways, postal services, radio, telephones, and telegraphs, covered its cultural and educational expenditures, its public services, and its administration of justice. If forty years ago, a region as disadvantaged as Bavaria could cover its

[177] In any case, the honest barter system will clean up the export market.

[178] Quoted by Juan Beneyto in **National Socialism**. Ed. Labor.

[179] See "*Finance and* Power" by J. Bochaca.

expenses and still have money left over to contribute to the payment of the national debt, and did so by implementing barely a quarter of its ideological program—which was necessarily subordinated to the political needs of the moment—it is breathtaking to imagine what a Lombardy, an Alsace, a Rhineland, a Kent, a Scotland, a Normandy, a Prussia, or a Holland might achieve in the Europe of the future...

The National-European Economy is based solely on reality. It recognizes that the state—regardless of its political orientation—is a poor businessman. Hence the repeated and resounding failure of all the misnamed "socialisms." If the State devotes itself to its functions—which are not to negotiate, nor to trade, nor to "open markets," but rather to maintain public order, ensure justice prevails, aid in the development of wealth, preserve the ecological environment, and prevent abuses of every kind— the State itself and the entire Nation will be able to devote the full measure of their energies to their proper functions, which are none other than the actualization and realization of the National Idea—[180] —in the realm of Foreign Policy, and the dissemination of Culture and Art in that of Domestic Policy.

We already sense that this prospect of a gradual reduction in taxes until they are ideally abolished will elicit a skeptical smile from most people. We will limit ourselves to recalling the case of Germany, which, we repeat, by implementing a minimal part of its program between 1933 and 1939, was the only country in the entire history of the world to substantially reduce its taxes while improving its public services and dramatically increasing national income. The main reason for taxes lies in government debt to the banking system, whether national or international. On the other hand, it is evident that profligate modern democratic states incur excessive spending on their expensive and ineffective "social" programs, which would be better provided by private entities—approved, of course, by the State—with purposes perhaps less "social," but endowed with the efficiency and productivity inherent in the individual initiative of the people of our Europe.

The state does not need to borrow money from anyone. If it needs to renew the armed forces' weaponry, all it must do is place the corresponding orders with its military equipment factories and pay with banknotes issued by the Mint. To those who are outraged, claiming that

[180] Francis Parker Yockey: "*Imperium*," Omnia Veritas Ltd.

this is inflation, we will simply reply that it is far more inflationary to continue with the current system, which consists of paying off that debt by taking out a bank loan, which must be repaid with hefty interest added. On the other hand, labeling the renewal of the Army's arsenal or the establishment of a museum as "inflationary spending"—or, in other words, "unproductive"—is as absurd as claiming that an individual is squandering their money when they buy a set of exercise equipment or purchase a few books.

* * *

We have stated—and believe we have demonstrated—that state issuance and public (that is, likewise state) control of Money are indispensable for the management of a healthy economy; the Economy of the Future Europe. The third point concerns the grounding of Money in the Labor Standard, which we may also call the Wealth Standard, in place of the current Gold Standard system. In the course of this study, we have already referred sufficiently to this point to consider it pointless to insist on demonstrating the fact that Money, an instrument of measurement and exchange, must be based on the subject upon which it acts—that is, Labor and the Wealth generated by it—and not on a commodity without any objective value, such as Gold.

Only an era such as the present one, in which the subversion of all values—moral and material alike—prevails, can accept the principle of the Gold Standard with hardly any discussion. When one observes that Picasso enjoys worldwide renown while Anglada Camarassa is a complete unknown; that everyone speaks of Marx and Freud while ignoring even the existence of Feder and Rosenberg; when a thief is called a kleptomaniac, a sodomite a member of "gay power," and a communist a "socialist," it should come as no surprise that a nation's wealth is considered to depend not on its labor, its resources, and the wealth produced by its inhabitants, but on the gold reserves stored in the vault of its Central Bank. The great success of the System's spin doctors has been to make people—, and even those supposedly belonging to the elites—believe that economics is an abstruse science, accessible only to the privileged minds of its exegetes, certified and approved by the System itself. Economics, certainly, may present aspects not easily understood by the so-called "man on the street," but what should be understandable to him—if he were to escape the collective brainwashing that the System has imposed on a global scale—is that it is impossible for wealth to depend on gold. that poverty is a consequence of abundance and that, "by extension," people must tighten their belts for having worked and produced too much.

And the fourth and final point concerns the acceptance, without mental reservations of any kind, of the principle that the Machine is a blessing for man, and not a curse. And that its purpose consists not in giving man work, but in taking it away from him, and in doing it better, faster, and cheaper.

For the Machine to adequately fulfill its role as Man's assistant, it is essential to fully grasp the natural function of Money, because if the Machine increases production and output but at the same time people do not have the necessary money to consume what is produced, then, instead of solving a problem, another one of massive proportions has been created. If Money serves to exchange the goods and services produced, and these have increased in volume, the amount of Money in circulation must increase proportionally. Many believe—because they have been led to do so by the hazy theories of our ineffable economists—that when there is a lot of money in circulation, the value of money decreases and uncontrolled inflation occurs. But let us not forget that money is a medium of exchange. A one-dollar bill, a peseta, or a mark is a token of a defined value. It represents a quantity of produced wealth, or of existing potential wealth (in the case of the valuation of human wealth in National Accounts). As long as it represents a defined quantity of wealth or work performed, its value, obviously, can never change, and both inflation and deflation will be impossible.

We must make all sectors of society aware that the economy, ultimately, consists of producers and consumers, and that if the latter do not have purchasing power proportional to production, the economy will never function properly—. We must accept the fact that our economy—or rather, our economic concepts—belong to the Stone Age. Indeed: the precarious conditions in which the world operated until Watt's invention forced people to proclaim certain social laws designed to ensure the survival of peoples; and, of these laws, the best known is the one that prohibits idleness. Everyone must work. No one is allowed to get something for nothing. Whoever does so is punished and called a thief. In reality, ancient society could not act otherwise, since it was compelled to do so by the scarcity of the era preceding the advent of the Machine. This fundamental law had to be imbued with divine authority. The Jews, in the Old Testament, were taught that God had said to Adam:

"You shall earn your bread by the sweat of your brow." The Christian version of this law was given by Saint Paul, when he stated: "If anyone will not work, neither shall he eat." Saint Paul, in his Epistle, was right; Jehovah, rebuking Adam over the apple incident, was right too. All the thoughtful thinkers who defended the fundamental law of forced human labor were right—until 1765. That was the year the Machine appeared, and they ceased to be right. Or, at least, they ceased to be absolutely right. Or else, let's see what's happening around us.

What's going on? Well, the fact is that this law is violated millions of times every day. It is violated when the state pays unemployment benefits; it is violated when it pays benefits to war veterans and to their widows and orphans; it is violated when shareholders receive their dividends; it is violated when members of cooperatives recover a portion of the money they have spent in one of their society's stores; it is violated every time a person inherits money. It is violated when retirees collect their pensions. In none of the cases cited has the money been earned through human labor. If anything, the labor necessary for the production of goods—which has caused worker unemployment and also made shareholders' dividends possible—has undoubtedly been performed, but it has been performed by machines. If it had not been done, we would be justified in denouncing the beneficiaries of unearned income and punishing them as idlers, leaving them without food, just as St. Paul advocated. But the fact is that the work has been done; and moreover, in a faster, more efficient, more rational, and easier way than before. What is more: we see that the number of unemployed is increasing with the progress of the Machine. The law of human forced labor has been shattered!... If only St. Paul had had the foresight to say: "If a man does not work, or the machine does not work for him, the man shall not eat..."

For, after all, what do we call work? The alienating task of millions of proletarians and office workers who are physically present in workshops and offices for eight or more hours, and then spend another two or three commuting back to their suburban homes, with a total—and forced—forgetfulness of the realization of their own personality? Do we call work something that must be done as a punishment imposed by Jehovah on the first man? And yet, could we not, rather, call work the creative talent of man, acting upon Nature through the Machine? Do we not believe that the time has come to replace the old, biblical "Work so that you may live" with the infinitely more dignified and appropriate for our age "Work and live"?

We do not advocate human inactivity, brought about by the Machine. Man will continue to work, first because he is a dynamic creature—at least Homo europeus—and not a static one; and second because there are countless things to do, both within our own territory and in other lands to which our creative ingenuity or the imperial instinct of the Idea may lead us. In short, the organization of "free time," won by the Machine for Man, no longer falls to the Digestive System of the Organism—the Economy—but to the Brain of the State. But what must be fully grasped is that there are other kinds of work besides those imposed by the fear of perishing from starvation. What this means is that human labor would no longer be indispensable for sustenance and the only honorable way to acquire goods and enjoy services.

The spectacle of Man redeeming himself, through his work—which the invention of the Machine has entailed tremendous spiritual, mental, and physical labor—from the punishment imposed upon him for his sin, devoting himself to the enjoyment of a secure life and using the time he has won from the god Cronos to realize his own personality (those who possess one) or to contribute, according to their means, to the common good—is something that certain men, who often boast of being progressive, refuse to approve of. For them, happiness is almost immoral. Nevertheless, these idolaters of the Past, with their clocks stopped in 1765, watch helplessly as the Machine triumphs, now the freedom of Man—despite the misuse he may have made of it at times—banishing the specter of Poverty forever.

* * *

We have said that the Law of Human Compulsory Labor, proclaimed by Jehovah and elaborated upon by Saint Paul, is violated daily. And it is natural that it is violated because, as Voltaire said: "If we cast it aside, it will return at a gallop." Both the dividends of the rich (securities, bonds, etc.) and the "dividends" of the poor (unemployment benefits; social security; birth premiums; family allowances, etc.) are flagrant violations of that archaic "Law." The idea that a person can receive money for work they have not personally performed may be condemned as much as one likes, but every day it spreads further, everywhere, in its practical application. In certain countries (Belgium, the Netherlands, Canada), workers whom machines—and other circumstances such as the current "Crisis"—have left unemployed receive eighty percent of their actual wages.

Facts are stubborn, as Pascal said. It is a fact that the "Law" is being circumvented, precisely because it no longer serves its purpose. The time has come to frankly admit that just as a human community must sometimes pay for the mistakes of its leaders, it is logical, natural, and just that it should benefit from the achievements of those leaders or the members of its elite. If Europe paid—and continues to pay—for the actions of the petty men who led Western democracies in 1939, why should it not benefit fully from the inventions of Watt and his successors?

We do not intend for the Economy of the Future Europe to be a tear-jerking, sentimental, and philanthropic pseudo-science that merely ponders how nice it would be if everyone were a millionaire. Nothing of the sort. Our Economy is, at the same time, a philosophy and an exact science. We agree with Spengler when he stated that "any mixing of abstract concepts such as 'social' with concrete realities such as price, cost, and merchandise results in a worsening of living conditions for the economically weaker classes"[181]. We do not believe that anything should be given away to anyone. It cannot be repeated often enough that the Machine is not manna that a paternal Jehovah has caused to fall from the sky. The Machine is ours; it is a more than legitimate inheritance. It is not a gift; it is the result of the effort, the work, the research, and the selfless obstinacy of European Man. And as long as we are men and not anonymous members of the Great Marxist-Capitalist Termite- ; as long as we are of the same lineage as Thales of Miletus and Euclid; Watt and Copernicus; Edison and Ford, we will be partners in the collective well-being that the Machine can provide; the Machine that is ours, everyone's. Do not the defenders of the "Law of Forced Labor" say that we must not get something for nothing? Or, in other words, that we must follow their outdated Law? Very well. Let us follow their reasoning and tell them that man would not enjoy the benefits of his Machine in exchange for nothing, for the simple and good reason that for centuries he has invented, perfected, and improved its performance, and then consumed the products it produced. What, then, do the orthodox seek? That man inherit only Jehovah's "curse" but not his own inventions?

Therefore, if Man is to benefit from his Machine, he must not only free it from the wretched prostitution imposed upon it by Finance, but

[181] Oswald Spengler: "*Decisive Years.*"

also from that imposed by the "Law of Forced Labor." For this reason, it is self-evident, it is axiomatic that if the Machine frees Man from a large part of his labor burden and at the same time increases Production in fantastic proportions, two measures must be adopted that complement one another:

1. Reduction of the workday.

2. Distribution of a National Dividend. Let us examine them.

The reduction in the workweek follows clearly, arithmetically, from the steady progress of the Machine, which far outpaces population growth and which, were it not for the combined constraints of the Law of Compulsory Labor and the financial cycles of the System, would outpace it by an incalculably greater margin. Moreover, considering that our Economy—the Economy of the Future Europe—is naturally subordinate to the higher Political Body of which it is a part, it is likely that the State will deem necessary a series of public works projects, not immediately profitable, which would slow the pace of the reduction in the workweek, thereby eliminating the potential social upheaval that an overly abrupt reduction would inevitably cause. Finally, we must also bear in mind that, by basing ourselves exclusively on facts and realities and not on "social" pipe dreams, such as the current Spanish labor legislation that indiscriminately prohibits free dismissal, we would finally put an end to the current degrading working conditions, especially in large cities, where so many factory and office workers kill time miserably, in mystical anticipation of quitting time[182], simply because the dense stupidity of the technocrats in our current economy has imposed the dogma of the eight-hour workday. When the reality is that it is enough for just four or five people to actually work. It has already been forgotten that at the beginning of the century there was a ten-hour, and even a twelve-hour, workday, and that while we have reduced the workday by thirty-three percent, our technological power has increased by five thousand percent. We do not mean to suggest that one should work only a few minutes because technical and economic progress also has its demands, but we believe that one need not be well-

---

[182] According to Maurice Mareuse in *"Le Contrôle de Gestion dans les Entreprises,"* the actual working time in France in 1938 was four hours in a typical factory. The remaining four hours were lost to downtime. Mareuse considered six and a half hours of actual work to be optimal productivity.

versed in mathematics; simple arithmetic suffices to understand that the reduction of the workday follows amply and irrefutably from technical progress.

Naturally, this raises the issue of leisure. A digression. We must sometimes be wary of semantics. The word "leisure" has, in Spanish, very pejorative connotations. The French word "loisirs," as an expression for "free time," is much more vivid and appropriate. In Spanish, we have nothing better than "leisure," an expression we use in its purely technical sense, representing the free time that the Machine provides to Man.

It is clear that the organization of leisure concerns both the economy and other state bodies. The prophets of extreme pessimism often object that leisure breeds idleness, vice, and crime. Nevertheless, Henry Ford observed that, by reducing his workers' workday from ten hours to just eight, most of them devoted themselves to their domestic "hobbies," sports, gardening, or hiking[183]. In 1923, a branch of the League of Nations published a study showing that alcohol abuse had decreased in industrial centers where the workday had been shortened. The entirely reputable League of Nations concluded that alcohol abuse and, in parallel, crime, were frequently the result of excessive work, since the worker, exhausted by the continuous effort required by long hours of work—or, if nothing else, by being on the job—is forced to seek relief from this stress by frequenting the tavern. The worker is happy to have the opportunity to improve his home, to exercise outdoors, and to be with his family. When the timid claim that workers should not be given so much free time on the grounds that they do not know how to use that freedom, one might reply that, for the same reason, people should be prohibited from swimming or participating in athletics, in order to prevent them from drowning or suffering a broken collarbone.

We have said, and we repeat, that the Organization of Leisure is the responsibility not only of the Economy, but of the other State Organs as well. The economy must limit itself to fulfilling its function as the digestive organ of culture. The rest is not its concern. Nevertheless, as an integral part of the cultural organism to which it belongs, the economy has an interest in the organization of leisure—or the free time that the machine leaves us, and will leave us more and more. There is

[183] Henry Ford: "*My Life and Work.*"

much, very much to be done: factories and workshops must be made more attractive. We have seen in Germany, Austria, Sweden, and northern France industrial facilities that, while certainly not architectural monuments, were at least attractive, clean, and surrounded by beautiful gardens. We must clear the countryside, thereby eliminating one of the main causes of forest fires. We must promote amateur sports. At a higher level, art must be fostered in its various forms. There is an endless array of things to do, to the point that the pejorative connotation generally associated with the word "leisure" can be discarded from now on. We have already said that "Homo Europeus" is a dynamic being, not a static one. He has a Faustian conception of life, and liberation from forced labor—replacing it with useful and formative work—will give new wings to his imagination and creative impulse. We have said it and we repeat it: the old formula of "Work to Live" can—and must—be replaced today by "Work and Live."

The material liberation of Man by the Machine necessitates, as we have already said, not only the reduction of the workday but also the distribution of a National Dividend. We are all shareholders in the powerful enterprise—in its economic aspect—Europe S.A. As shareholders, it is logical that we have the right to receive a dividend, just as when things go wrong, we must all contribute, willy-nilly, to the "capital increase," that is, to supporting our current mini-states—as fussy as they are incapable—by paying exorbitant taxes, including the "blood tax" that is usually levied without being "voted on" by any Parliament.

The National Dividend, moreover, justifies itself as a necessary alternative to the current unjust social security system, and, above all, to unemployment benefits. These unemployment benefits—unemployment caused in part by the constant improvement of the Machine—are, fundamentally, unjust. First of all, it exists not as a result of our current absurd economic system, but in spite of it, and to prevent it from collapsing. But, in any case, it is guilty of a double injustice: the first, that it comes from the pockets of those who are working; the second, that it cannot spare the recipient of such a benefit the humiliation of knowing where it comes from. There is, moreover, an additional drawback: it cannot prevent the creation of parasites who have not been driven from their jobs by the Machine, but by their own idleness. Thus, the current situation actually offers three solutions: the first consists of continuing to burden those who work with taxes in order to pay those who do not work; rewarding industriousness at the expense of idleness or the "misfortune" of progress brought about by a certain machine. The second consists of treating all scholars, inventors, technicians, engineers, and scientists—the Watts, Newcomens, Papins, Lavoisiers, Edisons, Faradays, and Otto Hahns—as undesirables, as public evildoers, for having committed the crime of lightening, through their marvelous achievements, the labor of their contemporaries. And the third and final solution consists of frankly acknowledging that those whom the Machine is leaving without work have the right to receive money to meet their needs, and, furthermore, to receive it in a way that is not a source of embarrassment or humiliation for them. Since it is obvious that neither the first nor the second alternative provides a satisfactory and dignified solution, we must accept the third. This third solution has the advantage of addressing all the country's inhabitants, whether they are workers or not. It takes into account what, for us, is an axiom: that the old notion that work is the only thing that entitles one to money must be supplemented by the idea that life itself generates a fundamental right to money.

We must never forget that, in economics, producers are just as important as consumers—not to mention that, within the labor force, we are all both producers and consumers at the same time. If, as is fundamentally imperative and necessary, a National Account[184] were maintained, the Annual Balance Sheet would be known with exact precision. And once the amounts allocated in the budget for the following fiscal year to investments in long-term public works, armaments, public education, etc., were deducted, the profit to be distributed among the shareholders of the corporation Europa S. en C. would be known. Naturally, nothing obliges us to distribute the entire profit among the shareholders. What would be economically fair and sufficient would be to distribute a minimum subsistence allowance to all inhabitants. Commander Douglas's studies[185], limited to Scotland, have shown that distributing just 2 or 3 percent of national profits would be sufficient to ensure a living wage he describes as "decent." And what

[184] This European National Accounts system should naturally reflect regional accounts. It is necessary to know what each partner has done, because although we all belong to the same enterprise and must cooperate and help one another, it is neither fair nor desirable that some should, in practice, have to constantly carry the burden of others. The distribution of the National Dividend should reflect, at least in part, the effort and contribution of each region.

[185] Ch. Douglas: "*Social Credit.*"

is considered such in Scotland would be regarded, at a minimum, as "quite good" in less-favored regions of Europe, such as Sicily, Ireland, Castile, or Karelia.

Is this possible? Arithmetically, it is not only possible but certain. Why? Because if, as in the case of the United States, the public debt is far greater than the entire value of the country, and the "fake" currency—that is, credit money—exceeds legal tender by eighteen times, and they manage to pay "fake" wages—unemployment benefits—to their inactive population, which amounts to 9 percent, we see that this 9 percent represents only one-eleventh of the total. So as long as 1/11 is greater than 1/18, this will be possible. Let us not forget that unemployment benefits are paid with real money, that is, with legal tender. In other words, 1/18 of the existing money is more than enough to pay one-eleventh of the producers who are forcibly unemployed. It is certainly true that these unemployed producers do not represent 11 percent of the country's total population, but it is no less true that there must necessarily be plenty of paper money left to cover the daily expenditures of all citizens throughout the country. In other words, by replacing the current counterfeit money with genuine, legal tender, we would have a money supply eighteen times larger, while a fraction of one-eighteenth of that supply—we repeat, a part of that one-eighteenth—is already enough to pay the counterfeit wages of eleven percent of a population in involuntary unemployment... And what is possible in the United States is equally possible in Europe, and especially in Spain, where the proliferation of banks has created a credit superstructure unparalleled in other neighboring countries[186].

We have said that, in our time, Life itself already confers a right to money, complementary to Work as the sole right to obtain money, according to the old concept, valid until Watt's invention. Every person, from the moment of their birth, must receive, as a shareholder of Europa S. en C., their corresponding share of the National Dividend. We consider it absurd and unjust that society should concern itself only with the sick, the mentally disabled, the elderly, and the unemployed. Do healthy, normal people who have not yet reached retirement age and

---

[186] In all fairness, it must be stated that Jewish surnames are not abundant in Spanish high-level banking, even though they also appear in positions of honor. But it must be borne in mind that finance is international by definition and that the specific weight of Spanish banking within the global context is disproportionately small.

who work not deserve to be cared for? Let us say that, at the very least, they deserve it just as much as the others. That is why we advocate for the elimination of the entire system of Social Insurance and Pensions, replacing it with the National Dividend, as a minimum standard of living, equal for all. The mere fact of implementing the National Dividend would practically demonstrate that Europe, Inc. was solvent, while the amount of the dividend would indicate the degree of prosperity of the European Nation. Furthermore, the National Dividend would prevent the State from harming those it should reward, nor would it reward those it should punish. By keeping its National Accounts in order, it would succeed in keeping its Economy in order.

Naturally, a certain degree of prudence and common sense would be necessary, especially in the initial years, so that the first dividends to be distributed would be low—as low as possible—covering only the bare minimum for survival[187].

We are aware that for the eternal pessimists, the mere idea of a National Dividend—even without specifying its scope or amount—irresistibly leads them to believe that in any country where such an idea were accepted, work would cease ipso facto and everyone would lie down in a hammock. To this we can respond as follows:

First.—Even if this were to happen, and the State were to tolerate it, it would last only a very short time, for the National Dividend would diminish or cease entirely as soon as the result of the next National Balance Sheet appeared negative, that is, in deficit. And with no profits, there would be no dividends.

Second.—The very nature of human beings belies the predictions of the eternally timid. The author recalls that, eight years ago, he received 350 francs a month in France, where he then resided, in the form of Family Benefits, for his three children and wife at home. With that amount, at that time, one could live in France; without extravagance, of course, but it would cover a minimum standard of living[188].

[187] Obviously, the determination of that minimum subsistence level would be a political matter, to be decided by the State after consulting with the relevant agencies, such as statistical institutes, etc.

[188] Those family benefits were, even then, far higher than that figure, not to mention the numerous services provided by the State, such as free education, discounts on public

Nevertheless, I never felt like a slacker or a freeloader for receiving that monthly allowance, and I worked my eight hours—or more—exactly as I would have if I hadn't received it, even though I knew that receiving it barely covered my needs, and I was aware that such financial strain would turn into distress if I stopped working and claimed unemployment benefits. When I have nothing special to do—which is not common—I make a point of finding something to occupy myself with, because activity is inherent to the human species, and especially to Europeans. In other words, without being particularly passionate about money—far from it—eight years ago I was just as eager to earn 5,000 francs a month as if I had never seen those 350, and I remain just as eager to earn them in Spain, where I no longer receive, in Spain, those 350 francs or any amount even remotely similar, in pesetas. But I would have appreciated that pension then, and I would appreciate it today, because knowing that I and my family are safe from the risk of going hungry spares me endless worries and allows me to work better. If anything, the only thing that might bother or upset me about the current social pension system is knowing that my pension has to come out of the pockets of all taxpayers, including myself.

In short, the man who doesn't care whether he earns 350 or 5,000—no matter how "idealistic"[189] or self-righteous he may claim to be—does not exist. He is not of this world, and this book was not written for him. He may be a Martian, or better yet, a lunatic, but we doubt he is an earthling and we resolutely deny that he is a European. But the fact is, we also believe that this is approaching the matter by observing the human perspective from the basement window, at ground level, because it means refusing to take into account something very subtle, yet very real: the creative impulse of the European Man. The prophets of the hammock, with their pessimism and their thick glasses in tow, forget that Man—who certainly has a Body—also has a Soul, an agonizing creative impulse to go "beyond," that divine breath that some call inspiration, others a thirst for progress, and which everyone possesses subconsciously, with or without a name. There is so much to do in the World, so much to do in Europe, that we can rule out the danger of the hammock, at least for the coming millennium. We have genuine

---

transportation fares, etc.

[189] It is evident that Mussolini, with his robust humanity, was infinitely more idealistic than the scrawny Stalin. Idealism has nothing to do with the austerity of puny ethnic groups; a fact so obvious that it must be constantly repeated to certain fools.

national embarrassments, such as Extremadura with its aridity and backwardness, in Spain; Corrèze, with its neglect and isolation, in central France; the steppes of our Monegros; the poverty of Calabria, in southern Italy; the centuries-old neglect of Ireland... We have projects as old as they are urgent, such as the Channel Tunnel, which, by connecting England with the Continent, will undoubtedly and once and for all contribute to an understanding and a bond between us that should never have been broken; such as the Rhine-Danube-Rhône Canal; such as the urgent opening of new Pyrenean passes between France and Spain; such as the ecological protection of our European homeland... With the payment of the National Dividend, that work would be done, not just as well as it is done today, but much better for the simple reason that a job well done would logically result in a larger dividend, and thus everyone would have a personal stake in the results. This, moreover, would help put an end once and for all to the old and foolish hostility between Machine and Labor, for since the amount of the National Dividend would depend on the increase in real wealth, it would forever end the suspicion that Labor feels toward any machine that saves on labor. Greater efficiency in work would produce better results, and these would generate a larger dividend to be distributed among all.

* * *

In summary, then, the Solution to the current "Crisis," viewed from a European perspective, boils down to the four points analyzed above, namely:

a) Replace private control of money with national control.

b) Make the State the sole issuer of Money, basing that issuance on the volume of goods and services produced by the Community, and which that same Community must consume.

c) Replace the Gold Standard with the Labor Standard, or, more precisely, with the Wealth Standard.

d) To recognize that labor entitles one to receive money to live well, but that it is not the sole source of the right to money, since life also confers an essential right to money, and for this reason the National Dividend must be established.

This is the essential point. The rest is a matter of circumstance, of mere detail. We have already outlined some practical methods for the rational application of each of the points mentioned. We have stated that the replacement of the current Credit Money with Real Money, free from the inherent flaw of Debt, should be done gradually. That the issuance of the new sound money would be based, at the same time, on information technology and on data from the National Balance Sheet. That the dethronement of Gold could be done almost overnight, harming no one but international speculators. And that the amount of the National Dividend should ensure a minimum standard of living to be determined by the State. We need only add that the issuance of sound money, carried out, naturally, by the Mint, would solve the problem of its circulation in three possible ways.

a) Through public works and other government expenditures, such as arms procurement, nature conservation, public education spending, etc.

b) Through the granting of interest-free loans to companies that sufficiently demonstrate the need for them.

c) Through the institution of the National Dividend. Naturally, the Economy of New Europe should sweep away all the archaisms of the current Capitalist Economy and its false opposite, Marxism, or State Capitalism. Trade unions, whatever their political stripe, must be consigned to the Pantheon of Oblivion, as anachronistic, ineffective, and unjust[190]. At heart, they are all based on the Class Struggle, conceivable, if not excusable, in the era of the dawn of the Machine, in Dickens's England, and in the tendentious exaggerations of the great-great-grandfather Marx, a bon vivant who never worked a day in his life, a failure and a man of resentment, harboring messianic hatreds against a Society he could not comprehend. So many books have already been written refuting Marx's errors that we do not believe it is worth dwelling on this point any further. To criticize, today, Marx's abstruse and convoluted theories is, in fact, counterproductive, for it is to grant them a status they neither have nor have ever had. Marxism has been discredited by facts and by history. It has been discredited by life, and if it persists—with a thousand anti-Marxist patches that allow it to survive—in the USSR, it is thanks to the colonial exploitation of its wretched Eastern European satellites and the aid that the U.S., the UN, and other institutions of the so-called Free World provide it daily. Without this, it would have collapsed long ago.

---

[190] "Trade unionism, always and in every age, has ended up being a lackey of Big Capital—not industrial capital—and an exploiter of both the employer and the worker," Oswald Spengler: "*The Decline of the West.*"

Along with the unions, the charitable institutions invented to mitigate the failure of capitalism—such as Social Security, Unemployment Insurance, Family Benefits, etc.—must disappear, albeit gradually. All of this must be fully replaced by the National Dividend. And if the State deems that exceptions based on time or place are necessary, it must naturally apply them, though on an exceptional basis and making it very clear that this is a temporary exception, motivated by such-and-such a reason. Obviously, this is not about prohibiting Charity, an evangelical virtue that deserves our utmost respect; Charity that will always exist and will always be justified because men are imperfect and unequal. But what cannot be done is to institutionalize it. Compulsory charity bears too close a resemblance to Bolshevism. Its practice, in any case, is not the mission of the State, but of the Church. Here it is worth recalling the words of Christ: Give to God what is God's, and to Caesar what is Caesar's. With its obsession with meddling in everything and regulating everything, the modern democratic state has come to regard itself as God the Father. It! So agnostic!

* * *

And that's all, my dear reader, who has done me the honor of following me all the way to the end. I am aware that what I have set forth above could have been presented in a more obscure, esoteric, and complicated manner. If I have explained it in a simple and direct way, it has been out of respect for you and for myself, because if there is one thing that writings on economics suffer from, it is a tendency toward logomania, the purpose of which may be, perhaps, to conceal their emptiness. I have not presented you with an optional vision of Europe's economic future; you and I have traveled together along the path of Common Sense, which—like the courage of recruits in the Army—is assumed of everyone. I have not proposed an option based on the classic approach of the Liberal school: this is better and this is worse, with all due respect to those who disagree. I have told you, I have shown you, and I hope I have convinced you that the Labor Standard must replace the Gold Standard, that the State must be the sole issuer of currency, and that, in economics, false charity must be replaced by justice. And there is no choice. Either a National-European Economy, or the collapse of Europe, in the very short term. Naturally, the Economy of Common Sense can only be implemented by a specific political regime. The solution is, above all, political. But this, as Kipling would say, is another story.

BIBLIOGRAPHY

-Mario Alberti. *The Body and Soul of Money.*

-Jacques Bordiot. *A Hidden Hand Directs...*

-Hector Brailsford. *Finance.*

-Stuart Chase. *Men and Machines.*

-Gilbert K. Chesterton. *England's Little History.*

-Maurice Colbourne. *Economic Nationalism.*

-Maurice Colbourne. *The New Economy.*

-Cesare Corti. The House of Rothschild.

-Henry Coston. *The Financiers Who Rule the World.*

-Henry Coston. *High Banking and Trusts.*

-Gertrude M. Coogan. *Money Creators.*

-A. Dauphin-Meunier. *Banking Through the Ages.*

-A. Dauphin-Meunier. *History of Banking.*

-Alexander Del Mar. *The Science of Money.*

-Raymond D'Ivernois. *The Effects of the Continental Blockade.*

-Charles Douglas. *The Control and Distribution of Production.*

-Charles Douglas. *Social Credit.*

-Edouard Drumont. *Jewish France.*

-Sheldon Emry. *Billions for the Bankers. Debts for the People.*

-Gottfried Feder. *The Struggle Against High Finance.*

-Gottfried Feder. *The German State on a National and Social Basis.*

-A. N. Field. *The Truth about the Slump.*

-Henry Ford. *The International Jew.*

-Henry Ford. *My Life and Work.*

-Anatole France. *The Red Lily.*

-Felix J. Frazer. *The ABC of Money.*

-Hector Leslie Gantt. *The Gantt System.*

-Pierre Gaxotte. *The French Revolution.*

-Vicente Gay. *The National Socialist Revolution.*

-Hermann Hoffmann. *Prince Bismarck.*

-C. K. Howe. *Who Rules America?*

-Arthur Kitson. *A Fraudulent Standard.*

-Las Cases. *Memorial of Saint Helena.*

-G. H. Lebesque. *Social Credit and Catholicism.*

-Arnold S. Leese. *Gentile Folly.*

-Lloyd Lewis. *Myths After Lincoln.*

-Charles A. Lindbergh, Sr. *Banking and Currency and the Money Trust.*

-Ferdinand Lundberg. *America's Sixty Families.*

-Louis Madelin. *The Revolutionaries.*

-R. Mc Nair Wilson. *Promise to Pay.*

-R. Mc Nair Wilson. *God and the Goldsmiths.*

-R. Mc Nair Wilson. *The Bankers' Conspiracy.*

-Jules Michelet, *History of France.*

-Eugene de Mirecourt. *Rothschild.*

-Richard R. Morrisson. *The Paradox of Capitalism.*

-Eustace Mullins. *A Study of the Federal Reserve.*

-James C. Oliver. *A Treatise on Money.*

-Thomas Porter. *The Green Magicians.*

-Angelo S. Rappoport. *Pioneers of the Russian Revolution.*

-R. E. Search. *Lincoln: The Martyr.*

-G. Bernard Shaw. *The Apple Cart.*

-Frederick Soddy. *Citadel of Chaos.*

-Wycliffe B. Vennard. *Conquest or Consent...?*

-Vincent C. Vickers. *Economic Tribulation.*

-Nesta H. Webster. *Secret Societies and Subversive Movements.*

-Francis Parker Yockey. *Imperium.*

-J. Bochaca. *Finance and Power.*

-J. Bochaca. *The History of the Vanquished.*

-Juan Beneyto. *National Socialism.*

-Cornelius Carl Veith. *Citadel of Chaos.*

-Maurice Mareuse. *Management Control in Businesses.*

-Oswald Spengler. *Decisive Years.*

-Oswald Spengler. *The Decline of the West.*

-and Encyclopædia Britannica, CEDADE Bulletins, etc.

Other books published by Omnia Veritas

OMNIA VERITAS
Omnia Veritas Ltd presents:
Fatima
and the
GREAT CONSPIRACY
DEIRDRE MANIFOLD
Fatima
and the
GREAT CONSPIRACY
This meant creating, or making, money out of nothing, being allowed to call it money, and to lend it to the public at a high interest rate.
This private syndicate acquiring a cast-iron monopoly over the supply and circulation of the money not just of England, but of the whole world...

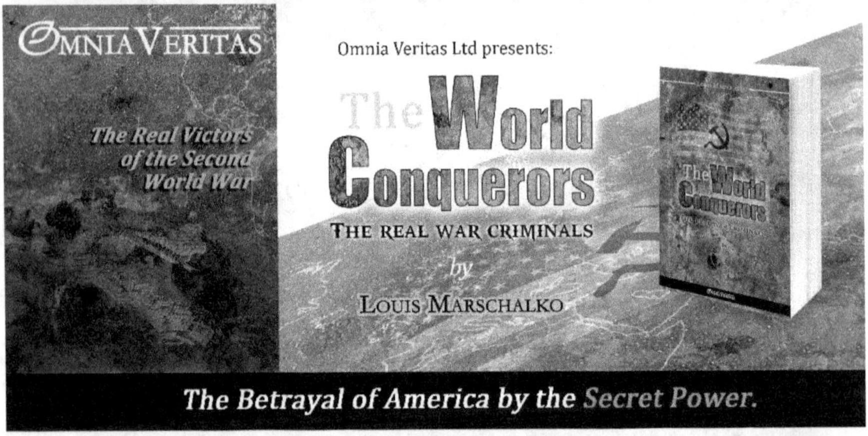
OMNIA VERITAS
The Real Victors of the Second World War
Omnia Veritas Ltd presents:
The World Conquerors
THE REAL WAR CRIMINALS
by
LOUIS MARSCHALKO
The World Conquerors
The Betrayal of America by the Secret Power.

OMNIA VERITAS
OMNIA VERITAS LTD PRESENTS:
UNINTENDED
CONSEQUENCES
A gripping action-thriller and historical fiction work centered on American gun culture and gun rights
2ND AMENDMENT
1789
PROTECT YOURSELF
JOHN ROSS
We the People
UNINTENDED
CONSEQUENCES

OMNIA VERITAS
Historians are finding less and less to celebrate about the Revolution...
Omnia Veritas Ltd presents:
THE FRENCH Revolution
A Study in Democracy
by
NESTA WEBSTER
An account of the bloody terror, the mob violence, and the overthrow of French religious tradition...
Hard political and historical facts compiled in this essential classic!

OMNIA VERITAS
"There was a class of persons who very well understood each other's interests, who very likely were related by racial and religious custom, and whose supra-nationalism transcended all city boundaries and borders of states."
Omnia Veritas Ltd presents:
The Babylonian Woe
by
DAVID ASTLE
"Yesterday it was a conspiracy against the men of a city, or a relatively small state; today a conspiracy against the whole world."
David Astle's masterpiece in a brand new edition!

OMNIA VERITAS
The meaning of Monarchy's struggle against the Money Power
Omnia Veritas Ltd presents:
Monarchy
Money
POWER
by
ROBERT MCNAIR WILSON
A master-piece of history
The true nature of Kingship revealed!

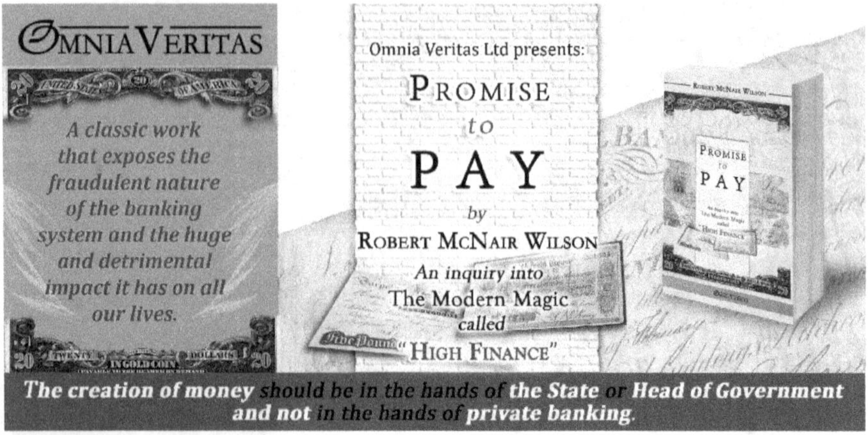
OMNIA VERITAS
A classic work that exposes the fraudulent nature of the banking system and the huge and detrimental impact it has on all our lives.
Omnia Veritas Ltd presents:
PROMISE to PAY
by
ROBERT MCNAIR WILSON
An inquiry into The Modern Magic called "HIGH FINANCE"
The creation of money should be in the hands of the State or Head of Government and not in the hands of private banking.

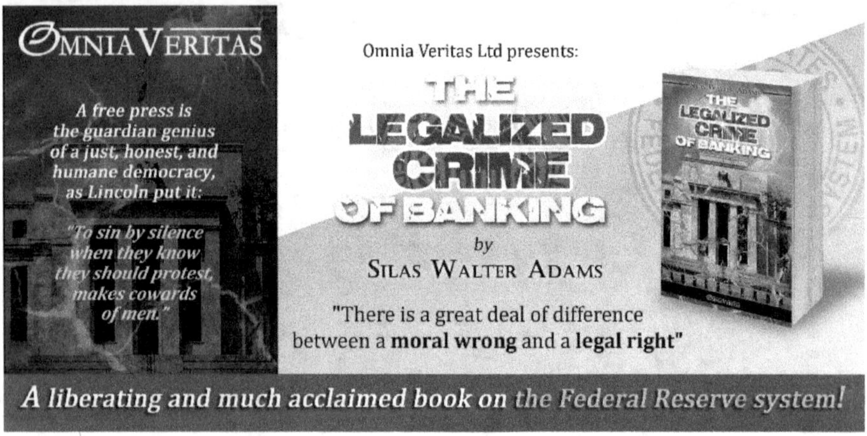
OMNIA VERITAS
A free press is the guardian genius of a just, honest, and humane democracy, as Lincoln put it:
"To sin by silence when they know they should protest, makes cowards of men."
Omnia Veritas Ltd presents:
THE LEGALIZED CRIME OF BANKING
by
SILAS WALTER ADAMS
"There is a great deal of difference between a moral wrong and a legal right"
A liberating and much acclaimed book on the Federal Reserve system!

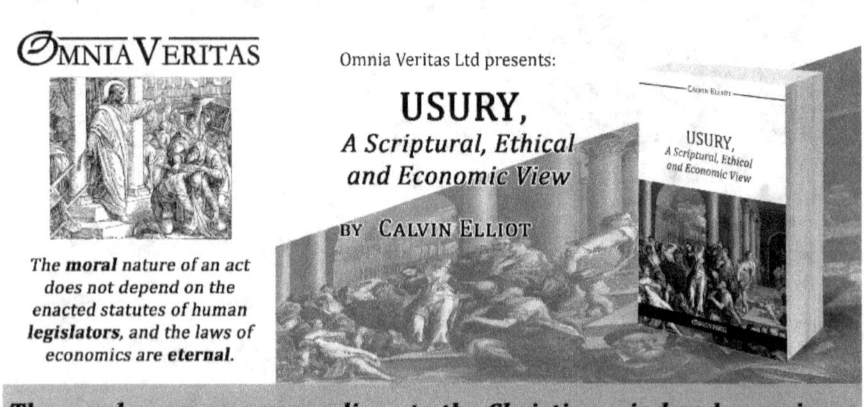
OMNIA VERITAS
The moral nature of an act does not depend on the enacted statutes of human legislators, and the laws of economics are eternal.
Omnia Veritas Ltd presents:
USURY,
A Scriptural, Ethical and Economic View
BY CALVIN ELLIOT
The word usury was very odious to the Christian mind and conscience

OMNIA VERITAS
OMNIA VERITAS LTD PRESENTS
THE DISPOSSESSED MAJORITY
THE DISPOSSESSED MAJORITY
THE TRAGIC AND HUMILIATING FATE OF THE AMERICAN MAJORITY

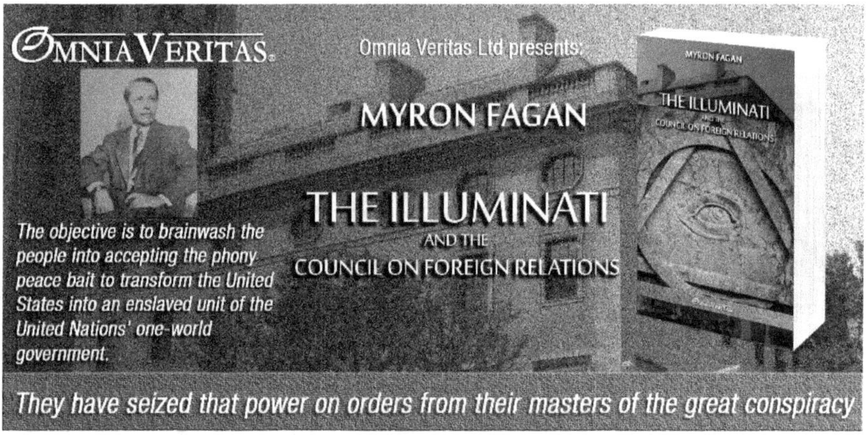
OMNIA VERITAS
Omnia Veritas Ltd presents:
MYRON FAGAN
THE ILLUMINATI
AND THE
COUNCIL ON FOREIGN RELATIONS
The objective is to brainwash the people into accepting the phony peace bait to transform the United States into an enslaved unit of the United Nations' one-world government.
MYRON FAGAN
THE ILLUMINATI
They have seized that power on orders from their masters of the great conspiracy

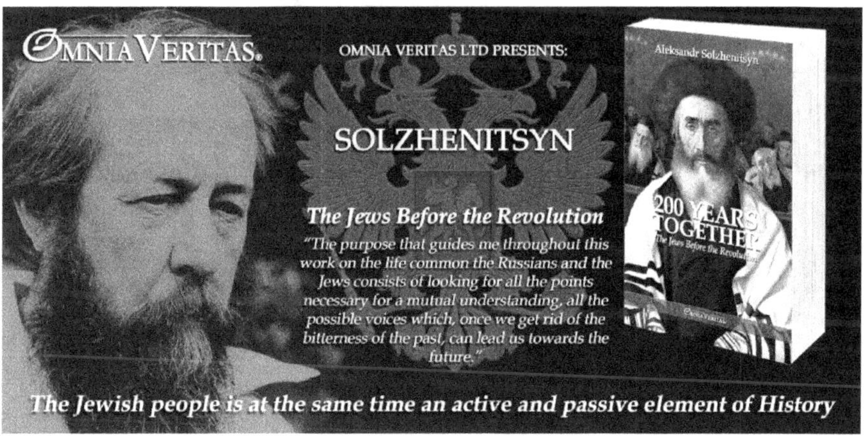
OMNIA VERITAS
OMNIA VERITAS LTD PRESENTS:
SOLZHENITSYN
The Jews Before the Revolution
"The purpose that guides me throughout this work on the life common the Russians and the Jews consists of looking for all the points necessary for a mutual understanding, all the possible voices which, once we get rid of the bitterness of the past, can lead us towards the future."
Aleksandr Solzhenitsyn
The Jewish people is at the same time an active and passive element of History

OMNIA VERITAS
OMNIA VERITAS LTD PRESENTS:
THE BROKEN CROSS
The Hidden Hand in the Vatican
Civilisation declines when reason is turned upside down, when the mean and the base, the ugly and corrupt, are made to appear the norms of social and cultural expressions...
THE BROKEN CROSS
The Church created our civilisation

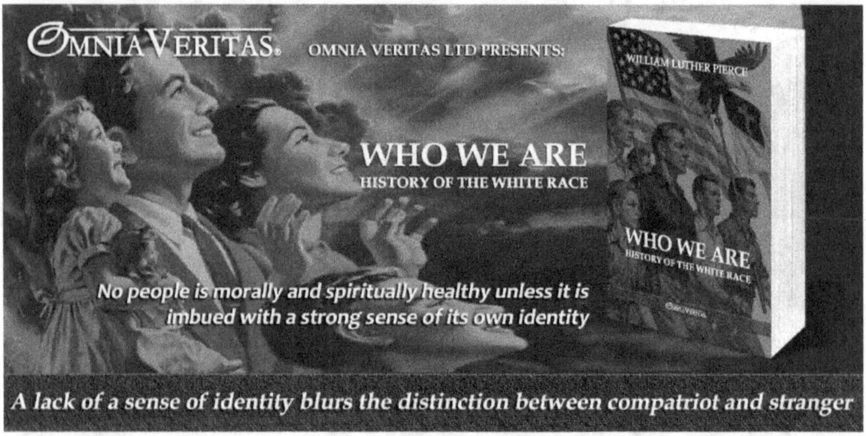
OMNIA VERITAS
OMNIA VERITAS LTD PRESENTS:
WILLIAM LUTHER PIERCE
WHO WE ARE
HISTORY OF THE WHITE RACE
WHO WE ARE
HISTORY OF THE WHITE RACE
No people is morally and spiritually healthy unless it is imbued with a strong sense of its own identity
A lack of a sense of identity blurs the distinction between compatriot and stranger

OMNIA VERITAS
OMNIA VERITAS LTD PRESENTS:
THE WALL $TREET TRILOGY
BY
ANTONY SUTTON
"Professor Sutton will always be remembered by his great trilogy: Wall St. and the Bolshevik Revolution, Wall St. and the Rise of Hitler, and Wall St. and FDR."
ANTONY SUTTON
THE WALL $TREET TRILOGY
This is a trilogy describing the role of the American corporate socialists known as the Wall Street financial elite

OMNIA VERITAS
LIGHT-BEARERS OF DARKNESS
This book is an attempt to show, by means of documentary evidence, that the actual world conditions are under the influence of mystic and secret societies through which the Invisible Centre is seeking to direct and dominate the nations and the world.
LIGHT-BEARERS OF DARKNESS

OMNIA VERITAS
THE TRAIL OF THE SERPENT
An attempt to trace the worship of the ancient Serpent, the Creative Principle, the God of all initiates of the Gnostics and Cabalists, emanating from the Hellenised Jews of Alexandria.
THE TRAIL OF THE SERPENT

OMNIA VERITAS
Omnia Veritas Ltd presents:
THE SECRETS OF THE FEDERAL RESERVE
by
EUSTACE MULLINS
HERE ARE THE SIMPLE FACTS OF THE GREAT BETRAYAL
THE SECRETS OF THE FEDERAL RESERVE
THE LONDON CONNECTION
Will we continue to be enslaved by the Babylonian debt money system?

OMNIA VERITAS
OMNIA VERITAS LTD PRESENTS:
THE EUSTACE MULLINS COLLECTION
MURDER BY INJECTION
THE CURSE OF CANAAN
NEW HISTORY OF THE JEWS
THE SECRETS OF THE FEDERAL RESERVE
THE WORLD ORDER
EUSTACE MULLINS

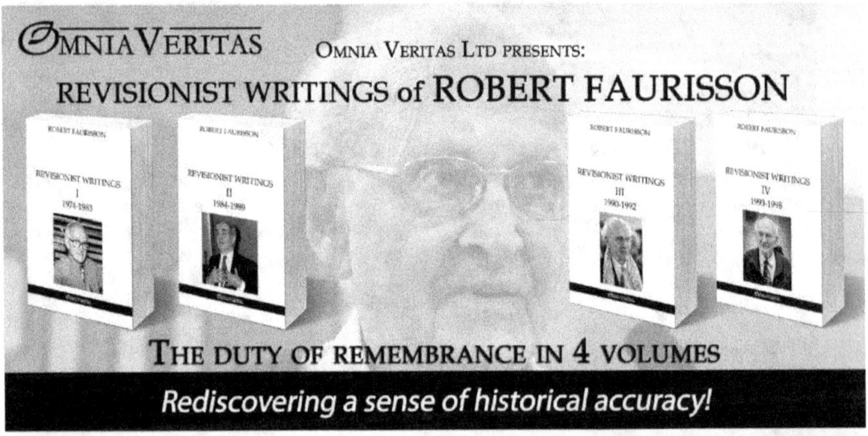
OMNIA VERITAS
OMNIA VERITAS LTD PRESENTS:
REVISIONIST WRITINGS of ROBERT FAURISSON
THE DUTY OF REMEMBRANCE IN 4 VOLUMES
Rediscovering a sense of historical accuracy!

OMNIA VERITAS®
www.omnia-veritas.com

www.ingramcontent.com/pod-product-compliance
Lightning Source LLC
LaVergne TN
LVHW052322200926
848481LV00002B/645